# GOD WANTS TO HEAL YOUR HEART

*A Book and Journal
to Help You Pray Inner Healing Prayer*

*To my dear friend, Sally, I love you, thank you for praying for the book.
Hebrews 6:10
Shade*

## BY SHADE O'DRISCOLL

*God Wants to Heal Your Heart: A Book and Journal to Help You Pray Inner Healing Prayer*

Trilogy Christian Publishers
A Wholly Owned Subsidiary of Trinity Broadcasting Network
2442 Michelle Drive, Tustin, CA 92780

Copyright © 2023 by Shade M. O'Driscoll

Scripture quotations marked (TLB) are taken from The Living Bible copyright © 1971. Used by permission of Tyndale House Publishers, Carol Stream, Illinois 60188. All rights reserved.

Scripture quotations marked (NLT) are from the New Living Translation Bible. Copyright© Used by permission of NavPress. All rights reserved. Represented by Tyndale House Publishers, a Division of Tyndale House Ministries.

Scripture quotations marked (NKJV) are taken from the New King James Version®. Copyright © 1982 by Thomas Nelson. Used by permission. All rights reserved.

Scripture quotations marked (NIV) are taken from the Holy Bible, New International Version®, NIV®. Copyright © 1973, 1978, 1984, 2011 by Biblica, Inc.™ Used by permission of Zondervan. All rights reserved worldwide. www.zondervan.com. The "NIV" and "New International Version" are trademarks registered in the United States Patent and Trademark Office by Biblica, Inc.™

For information, address Trilogy Christian Publishing Rights Department, 2442 Michelle Drive, Tustin, CA 92780. For information about special discounts for bulk purchases, please contact Trilogy Christian Publishing.

Trilogy Christian Publishing/ TBN and colophon are trademarks of Trinity Broadcasting Network.

*Trilogy Disclaimer: The views and content expressed in this book are those of the author and may not necessarily reflect the views and doctrine of Trilogy Christian Publishing or the Trinity Broadcasting Network.*

10 9 8 7 6 5 4 3 2 1
Manufactured in the United States of America
Library of Congress Cataloging-in-Publication Data is available.

ISBN: 979-8-88738-369-9
ISBN: 979-8-88738-370-5 (eBook)

I was so blessed reading your book, and I'm thrilled it will get "out there" because it will help so many.

Your true self—the one who is firmly planted in God's life and utterly filled with His love and excitement in His plans—comes through in a profoundly encouraging way. Although you make God's healing work very accessible, you're at the same time leading us to a very deep well.

My faith was kindled, I was washed by wave after wave of God's love, and my eyes were lifted to greater possibilities in knowing Him and sharing His goodness.

I especially loved the way you talked about our sexuality and the marriage relationship—you were clear and dignified, gracious and uplifting. I have friends who suffered terrible abuse, and I can imagine this book making them feel safe about coming closer to Jesus where they've been so hurt and violated.

You are a gift, this book is a gift, and I am so grateful it can be a channel of God's healing flow!

—Dr. Sarah Colyn, PhD, Clinical Psychology
Vice President, Ministries of Pastoral Care

Shade O'Driscoll is a very loved and treasured friend and encourager to me and has decades of wisdom and experience in the field of Inner/Soul Healing prayer. I honor her as the original Co-founder of the 'Emotionally Free' prayer ministry, further developed by Rita and Dennis Bennett of Christian Renewal Association Inc, which I now lead.

In this wonderful journal, Shade and the Holy Spirit lead you through a gentle but very real and honest journey of deep personal healing of your hidden self, the one you have possibly been hiding because of guilt and shame. Through teaching, examples, and prayer, Shade reveals to us that God's love and mercy can truly conquer all, and that the Lord's presence can heal all your wounds when you bring them into His light and love.

I highly recommend you purchase this inner healing book with journal as soon as possible and begin your own healing journey of freedom!

—Diana Ingle,
CEO, Christian Renewal Association

Shade O'Driscoll, a longtime friend, was instrumental in leading me into the Baptism of the Holy Spirit in the late 1960s. It was a life changer and now has gone around the world through Aglow International, as well as many other avenues. I am eternally grateful for Shade's influence in my life.

As long as I've known Shade, she has always been about seeing a hurting heart and bringing healing and peace. In her new book, *God Wants to Heal Your Heart*, many will find the healing they have longed for their entire life. Written with clarity as directed by Holy Spirit, I am confident that all who dig into the truths Shade shares will come to a newfound place of freedom from past wounds and hurts. Adding the brilliance of journaling as one reads will enable each person to individually hear Holy Spirit bring healing to places they may have never recognized. Whom the Son sets free is free indeed, John 8:36.

—Jane Hansen Hoyt,
President, Aglow International

When Shade speaks, I listen! Coming from a wealth of Charismatic Renewal experience, it is good to ponder her reflections that we may be both informed and more fully conformed to the image of Christ. Shade shows why and how she has seen God "heal hearts" and the ongoing need for this. Combining journaling with reading is a means of personal pilgrimage which cannot but overspill into the lives of others. Thank you, Shade, for committing pen to paper.

—Archbishop Sean E. Larkin,
The United Anglican Church Province II

My very early childhood involved alcoholic, abusive parents. My dad died when I was four. My three siblings and I were placed in foster homes for fourteen years. I experienced sexual abuse by a hired man.

At age thirty-two, I met Shade O'Driscoll and we became great friends. She prayed inner healing prayers with me over the years. I benefited greatly as I know you will when you apply the truths of Shade's teaching in this book.

—Fran Lance,
author of *Tell Your Secret*, speaker, and Bible teacher

Many leaders who establish foundational ministries leave a legacy for generations. Shade O'Driscoll is one who stands tall in establishing a ministry of healing hearts and lives. While Rector of St. Luke's Episcopal Church, Seattle—the Mother Church of the Charismatic Renewal Movement—I saw first-hand the impact of the ministry Shade, Rita Bennett and others led, seeing lives transformed and freedoms gained. This book relates the foundational principles of Inner Healing but goes well beyond. The text is a gentle invitation for readers to encounter the healing presence of our Lord through powerful testimony and prayerful engagement through journaling. This little book is dynamite, revealing the life-transforming power of God's love.

—The Reverend Dr. John Roddam,
Episcopal Priest (Retired)

*Changes have been made to protect the privacy of individuals whose stories are told in this book.*

*All biblical references and quotations which are not otherwise documented are from the King James Version of The Holy Bible.*

# DEDICATION AND ACKNOWLEDGMENTS

To those who prayed through the years for the writing of this book, you know who you are. Though late in coming as some might think, you didn't give up on me or on God. It is now His, and to Him and to you I dedicate it.

I thank my daughters, Mary and Joanna, and my grandson, Christof, who without their help on the computer, the book would not be.

# INTRODUCTION

God wants to heal your heart. God is for you not against you (Romans 8:31). You are special to God; you came from Him. You were made in His image (Genesis 1:26). There never has been and there never will be another you with the same spirit and the same soul. You are His beloved treasure. He loves you more than anyone could ever love you, and no one can take your place in His heart.

His love is unconditional love. It does not depend on you being good. God sent His Son, Jesus to heal your broken heart. "…He has sent Me to heal the brokenhearted…" (Luke 4:18). Psalms 34:18 (NIV) says the Lord is close to those who have a broken heart, and He will save those who are crushed in spirit.

Inner healing prayer allows God, as well as ourselves, to "set aright" or "make well" those things which have gone wrong in our lives; those things which have happened to us or by us which were against our Father God's loving nature and will. We live in a fallen world where sin and evil, sickness and death reside, but God so loved the world that He sent Jesus, His Son, to us to redeem our lives, heal our hearts, and restore our souls.

The foundation of inner healing prayer rests upon the unshakable truth that GOD loves YOU and that LOVE can overcome anything that has happened or will happen to YOU. "For whatever is born of God overcomes the world. And this is the victory that has overcome the world—our faith" (1 John 5:4, NKJV). By our faith, when we pray inner healing prayer, we open a portal to God and invite Him to come into our lives and/or the lives of others and heal hearts.

God is love, and He is merciful. He heals hearts in many ways. He told me to write about inner healing prayer, because it's the way I have seen Him heal hearts. This is the way He taught me, but dear reader He can and may heal your heart in a most wonderful and unexpected way. Just know He wants to heal it because He's in love with you, and He longs for you to be in love with Him.

I learned how to pray this way through God's mercy because my own heart and the hearts of my family needed healing. I became an inner healing prayer counselor, and for over thirty-five years guided others in inner healing. I am writing this book so you too can know how to pray inner healing prayer for your heart to be healed.

This is not only a book to read and to pray, but also to use as a journal on the blank pages. Use it to write that which God does and tells you during your prayer times. It is necessary to journal because when you write what you feel or what you see God is doing and what He is saying to you, it is imprinted upon your heart and not easily forgotten.

I write about many different things that can go wrong in our lives, and how our Lord can bring forgiveness, reconciliation, deliverance, redemption, and restoration. Some of these things will have meaning in your life, others will not. You can just leave the journal pages blank which concern inner healing that is not appropriate to you.

In this life there are some situations which are so major, our hearts are left fragmented. One must hear from God Himself and be caught up in His Presence and love in order to have peace, to have an answer to the question "why," to live in forgiveness, and to be made whole again. That is what inner healing prayer is all about. It's prayer with the expectancy of experiencing one's heavenly Father or His Son, Jesus. It is in their Presence and love, that questions are answered, that good is victorious over evil, and that peace and wholeness come. As you commit to and devote the time it takes to pray inner healing prayers, you will be giving God the opportunity to do that which He longs to do—heal your heart.

—Shade O'Driscoll

# TABLE OF CONTENTS

Dedication and Acknowledgments. . . . . . . . . . . . xi

Introduction . . . . . . . . . . . . . . . . . . . . . . . . . . xiii

Chapter 1. When Does My Heart Need to Be Healed, and How Do Wounds Come?. . . . . 19

Chapter 2. Inner Healing Prayer: What Is It? . . . . . . 27

Chapter 3. Inner Healing Prayer: How Do I Pray It? . . . 35

Chapter 4. Stories of Hearts Being Healed . . . . . . 49
    The Woman Who Forgave Her Father. . . . . . . 55
    A Friend Facing Divorce . . . . . . . . . . . . . 58
    A Heart Who Loved Too Much . . . . . . . . . . 61
    A Man Caught in the Trap of Adultery . . . . . . 64
    The Woman Who Couldn't Forget Her Grandfather's Suicide. . . . . . . . . . . . . . 66
    The Artist Who Couldn't Paint . . . . . . . . . . 70
    A Lady Who Couldn't Face Authority. . . . . . . 78
    A Man Who Was Not Ready for His Heart to Be Healed . . . . . . . . . . . . . . . . . . . 86
    The Man Who Was Ashamed of His Ethnicity . . 89

Chapter 5. Inner Healing Prayer and Your Body . . . . 95

Chapter 6. Inner Healing Prayer and Your Soul and Spirit . . . . . . . . . . . . . . . . . . . . 121

Chapter 7. Inner Healing Prayer and the Baptism of the Holy Spirit . . . . . . . . . . . . . . . 133

Chapter 8. Inner Healing Prayer and Your Prenatal
       Months and Birth . . . . . . . . . . . . . . 145

Chapter 9. Inner Healing Prayer and Your Childhood
       Years . . . . . . . . . . . . . . . . . . . . . 153

Chapter 10. Inner Healing Prayer and Your Teen and
       Early Adult Years. . . . . . . . . . . . . . . 173

Chapter 11. Inner Healing Prayer for Your Children
       and Yourself as a Way of Life . . . . . . . . 177

About the Author . . . . . . . . . . . . . . . . . . . 185

Notes . . . . . . . . . . . . . . . . . . . . . . . . . . 187

# CHAPTER 1

# When Does My Heart Need to Be Healed, and How Do Wounds Come?

### *When does my heart need to be healed?*

If you are caught in an invisible net which keeps you reacting to or doing the same thing, which you wish you were not doing; or you are not able to do that which you need to do, then your heart needs to be healed. If you find yourself overreacting to normal situations, then your heart needs to be healed. When the traumas of your life, the sins of others against you, or sins you committed have caused you the inability to trust God or to trust and relate to others, then your heart needs to be healed. If God's good symbols of life have been changed to evil ones for you, such as persons or things in your life that were supposed to be good turned out to be bad, then your heart needs to be healed. If you are controlled by sins that you cannot stop committing or if you have a greater vulnerability to certain sins, then your heart needs to be healed. If you have a dislike of your body or self-hatred, then your heart needs to be healed. If you are immobilized by depression or fear, or have phobias, haunting memories, or unresolved anguish from the past, then your heart needs to be healed.

## *How do wounds come?*

Abuse and trauma including physical, emotional, or sexual cause your heart to hurt and wounds to come. Deprivation of love at any age can cause wounds, but most importantly infantile deprivation of a mother's love causes serious wounds with ramifications that may persist for a lifetime unless healed.

*Physical abuse*—such as beating in rage as a form of discipline or punishment by physical torture—wounds the soul as well as the body.

*Emotional abuse*, including rejection and shame by parents or others in authority, wounds the heart… especially a child's heart. Emotional trauma by abandonment at any age, by divorce or divorce of parents, by the death of either parent or a loved one, especially if the death is not expected, causes wounds in the soul and a hurting heart. A child's heart may feel rejected by a parent who dies.

When a child witnesses one parent abusing the other by physical abuse or verbal abuse, his or her heart becomes scarred. This can happen in insidious ways by the one parent devaluing, mocking, or putting down the other or simply arguing. The child's heart is torn between the two and feels compelled to choose sides and thus grows up with a distorted view of how God intended marriage.

Other emotional abuse could come from behavior that stems from the hatred of men or the hatred of and devaluing of women, minorities, or persons different from oneself. It could come from parents desiring their child to be the other gender or pressuring a child to fulfill their dreams, not allowing the child to make his or her own decisions.

If you were made fun of for being too fat, too thin, too tall, or too short, this is emotional abuse that bruises the heart. Anyone mocking, laughing at, or making fun of your body, your mind, or your personality as a child or an adult can wound the heart with an emotional memory that lasts a lifetime unless it is healed. This can happen with classmates, siblings, parents, extended family members, teachers, or other authority figures.

If an abortion attempt was made on your life, if you were conceived out of wedlock, or if you know your parents did not wish to have you whether you were adopted or not, then you may have the hidden hurt of not being wanted, like a slow emotional hemorrhage of the heart. If you had an abortion, your heart may be grieving over your lost child.

*Sexual abuse* including rape, sexual slavery, or simply being used for sex by anyone even in marriage wounds the soul and causes the heart to hurt. If you have used your sexual organs in ways God never intended, your heart can be heavy with wounds which you do not recognize. Misuse of our sexual organs can cause our self-identity as a child of God to be marred. If you have been the victim or the perpetrator in any of these situations, your heart needs to be healed.

The *traumas of life's circumstances* such as war, poverty, serious sickness, serious accidents, or major deprivation cause deep wounds in our hearts.

*Sin* causes the heart to hurt, and sin is that which is against what God intended, His loving will and purpose for you and all His creation. Sin came into the world by God's enemy and our enemy, Satan. So, we must remember at all times we are not dealing with flesh and blood, not even our own, but we are dealing with evil and the principalities of evil. "For we wrestle not against flesh and blood, but against principalities, against powers, against the rulers of the darkness of this world, against spiritual wickedness in high places" (Ephesians 6:12).

*Being exposed to violence or sins of all kinds and voluntary participation in sin as well as the major deprivations of life* mar the soul and cause the heart to hurt. This is not our Father God's will. He sent Jesus to heal our broken hearts, and that we might have life and have it more abundantly (Luke 4:18 and John 10:10). He has provided the way that we overcome and win against sin and Satan by the word of our testimony and the blood of the Lamb, and by our new life with God's Spirit in us (Revelation 12:11 and John 14:17).

The Lamb of God was, and is, Jesus. Our testimony is that which we say and believe in our heart (our faith) that Jesus's blood shed on the cross was for the forgiveness of all sin, the sin and any deprivation that we have suffered, as well as any voluntary participation in sin. The cross was, and is, Satan's total defeat. Through inner healing prayer, Jesus heals our hearts where sin and deprivation have wounded them.

God's word tells us to, "Stand therefore, having your loins girt about with truth, and having on the breastplate of righteousness…" (Ephesians 6:14). My hope is that this book will help you to know the truth about why your heart is hurting, and you will be able to put on your breastplate of righteousness which is Jesus's free gift to you.

On the cross in Jerusalem, He died so that all sin can be forgiven; past, present, and future, both ours and the sins whereby we've been a victim. Thus, He made it possible for our hearts to be healed, for you and me to have a redeemed and restored life. We've been made right with God, our Father. God accepted His Son's sacrifice on the cross for us by raising Him from the dead. Now we are like Jesus, God's son or daughter, and He is our Father. But in order for this to be a reality in our life, we must accept Jesus's free gift. We must accept that His blood shed on the cross paid in full our debt of sin. We must put on our breastplate of righteousness.

If you have never accepted what Jesus did for you, thank Him now for forgiving your sins and the sins of others which were committed against you. Invite Him to come into your heart (into your spirit) and be your Lord and Savior. He will come, and you can put on your breastplate of righteousness which He gives to you. You then can begin the journey with Him of getting your heart healed through inner healing prayer and standing strong in the truth of who you are, made righteous by Christ Jesus and a son or daughter of God (2 Corinthians 5:21). Hooray! He wants you healed, and you will be!

If you accepted for the first time Jesus's gift of the forgiveness of your sins, write about it. You are now a Christian, you don't have to be afraid of dying and going to Hell, Jesus will take you to Heaven to live forever with Him, Father, and Holy Spirit (who is now within you). Jesus has given you His righteousness and you've been made righteous by accepting it. Thank Him for the greatest and best gift that you have ever received!

Take some quiet moments and think about where your heart hurts and what caused it to hurt. Then write these thoughts on the blank page provided, or if you prefer, keep a journal other than this book. If you use the blank pages as your journal, make sure this book is not seen by others as well as any other journal, for you want your thoughts and prayers to be private.

Write what you want God to heal and anything you want to say to Him and anything He might say to you. This record will help you know what needs to be prayed in inner healing, and writing helps us to keep our minds focused when we are talking or listening to God. Also, when you journal your inner healing experiences with God, they become imprinted upon your soul and Satan cannot easily steal them away.

## *My Journal*

DATE:

*My acceptance and thanks to Jesus for His great gift to me. What caused my heart to hurt, and what I want God to heal.*

_____
_____
_____
_____
_____
_____
_____
_____
_____
_____
_____
_____

Chapter 1

# CHAPTER 2

# Inner Healing Prayer: What Is It?

What is inner healing prayer? It is inviting the Lord Jesus or your Father God (their Presence) to be known to you, known in a past, present, or future scene of your life. You ask Him to be in charge of what happened, what is happening to you, or what will happen to you or others. At the time of your pain, conflict, sadness, fear, or indecision you ask God to meet you there and for His will to be done in your life and the lives of others. This is possible because Father and Jesus have sent to us the Holy Spirit who is called the Spirit of Truth (John 16:1). It is Holy Spirit who makes known to our spirit what God wants to tell us, show us, or be to us.

Inner healing prayer is also asking our Lord, the Holy Spirit to make known to us something that we may have repressed which would be relevant to our healing. He may show us scenes that give meaning to the questions and wounds of our hearts.

As Holy Spirit remakes or makes the scenes from the movie of your life, you become aware of Father God's great love for you through His Presence with you. His will is done on earth (in the scene) as it is in Heaven. He is our Father; He is our God who redeems our life. If we give Him that which was hurtful to us, He will redeem it and turn it into good! His Presence heals our heart.

It is not something you make up by reasoning or thinking what God will do. You have sincerely asked Him, and He will come to you in thoughts, in mind pictures, in words, or in whatever unique way He communicates with you. You will be in touch with His Presence. He loves you. It is a real experience with your Lord Jesus or your Father God.

Your past is still available to God because He is outside of time. We are on a timeline; He is over time in the past, in the present, and in the future. Revelation 22:13 tells us that He is the beginning and the end, and He is the ever-present God in our present moments, "I Am that I Am" (Exodus 3:14).

In inner healing prayer He is able to rewrite the script of moments of your life on the parchment of your soul (on your mind and emotions). He redeems and rewrites what life's circumstances have written, what other people have written, what you have written, or what your enemy, Satan has written that has caused your heart to hurt. When in prayer by faith, you invite God to be Lord of your past, you are no longer captive to your past. He makes well your heart. What is impossible to man is possible to God (Luke 18:27).

God is love, God is good, and God is all powerful, His goodness overcomes evil. In inner healing prayer you experience His goodness (which is Himself) overcoming the evil, the sadness, and the loss in your life. We never know what He is going to do when we go into inner healing prayer because each person's life is different, and only He knows how to heal your heart. His Presence fills the hole with His tender love and takes away the ache. You then can be a part of His redeeming will for your life, happening on earth as it is in Heaven.

His Presence enables you to forgive others as well as yourself and if need be, to forgive Him for allowing certain things to happen. Once He told me, "Shade if I could have made it any different or easier for you, I would have." His tender love for me was so real. At that moment I knew He was absolutely trustworthy, and I understood how Job could say, "Though He slay me, yet will I trust in Him…" (Job 13:15).

Other people, family members, even strangers who have been involved in the scenes you experience in inner healing prayer will be touched for good. Because, in inner healing prayer you are giving God the opportunity to enter the history of your life and the lives of others who have been a part of your life and bring His redemption which effects changes for eternity. Inner healing prayer time is eternity time.

Once I was praying inner healing for a man who forgave his father for the abuse done to him when he was a child. In the inner healing scene with Jesus there, he, the child, was able to forgive the father. The father had never asked his son to forgive him; he had never owned up to the abuse. He lived in another state, but before the day was over, the phone was ringing. The father was calling, asking his son to forgive him. He knew nothing about the inner healing prayer, but in his spirit, he had been touched by God and set free by his son's forgiveness.

Jesus, through His shed blood on the cross, brings forgiveness of sin because He, Himself took the punishment for all sin when He was whipped and then crucified on the cross. He gives us the gift of forgiveness to give to those who have terribly wounded our souls or our bodies. In inner healing prayer He may show you Himself taking those very sins against you into His own body and soul on the cross. As you let them go into Him, He takes them, He suffers with them, He dies with them, He takes them to Hell; they are gone. You no longer have to carry them in your soul or body. You certify what Jesus did when you forgive the one who has hurt you. Then you are free!

He gives us the gift of forgiveness for ourselves. We can forgive ourselves for those things we are ashamed of, for those things we've done that have hurt others. He suffered and died with those sins too. In inner healing prayer you can turn away (repent) from your sins and ask Him to forgive you, and then you can forgive yourself. You don't have to go through life with hate and anger against others or yourself. "If we confess our sins (taking ownership and responsibility for them), He is faithful and just to forgive us our sins, and to cleanse us from all unrighteousness" (1 John 1:9).

Jesus won for us on the cross freedom in our minds, emotions, and wills from the terrible bondage that non-forgiveness causes us. He won freedom from sadness and a hurting heart. In inner healing prayer Jesus sets us free to enjoy the goodness of life that our Father God originally intended and intends for us now.

You do not have to deny what was done to you or what you did. God does not deny wrong or cover it up, but He will wash it away. Is there someone you need to forgive? Do you need to forgive yourself? Do you need to forgive God for allowing certain things to happen in your life? Remember, Jesus or Father will be there to help you. Write about the people you need to forgive including yourself or God.

# *My Journal*

## DATE:

*Those I need to forgive.*
*Things in my life that need to be washed away by Jesus's blood.*

We were made in God's image; our heart is like His heart (Genesis 1:26). Our heart was not made to know sin. Our Father is holy, He did not make our souls (minds, wills, and emotions) to know sin. We were not to know evil (Genesis 3:5).

In this present world sin assaults our souls and leaves wounds and scars on our hearts that only the Presence of Jesus or the Presence of Father can heal. Because He is holy, and He is love, "…God is love…" (1 John 4:16), He did away with sin once and for all on the cross. In His love, Jesus who knew no sin, took our sins and the sins of the whole world into His own body and died with them so our hearts would not hurt, and so we can have joy with Him now and in the life to come in Heaven (2 Corinthians 5:21).

Because we were made in God's image and because He is holy and we were made to be holy, we cannot bear evil. There are some things humans do to one another which we have experienced or seen that are so evil, we cannot bear it. It can cause us to have mental illness or be so depressed that we take our own life. But thank God, He has a way to deal with that kind of evil in inner healing prayer.

The prophet Isaiah had a vision of the Lord in Heaven with angels around about His throne. They were crying:

Holy, holy, holy, is the Lord of hosts…Then said I, Woe is me! …because I am a man of unclean lips, and I dwell in the midst of a people of unclean lips: …Then flew one of the seraphim unto me, having a live coal in his hand…he laid it upon my mouth, and said, Lo this has touched thy lips; and thine iniquity is taken away, and thy sin is purged (Isaiah 6:3, 6:5-7).

The live coal did not burn Isaiah's lips, it burned up the evil, so it was no more. In inner healing prayer we do not see God burning people. But we can ask Him to take evil from our minds and bodies as we have seen it or experienced it. We can then witness in inner healing His fire of the Holy Spirit taking the evil from our life as He took it from Isaiah's. We can also witness Him taking it out of persons who have manifested it.

If you have scenes of evil, haunting symbols of evil, or haunting emotions of evil in your mind that won't go away, in inner healing prayer you can give them to God. Make a basket with the palms of your hands and put the evil things one by one in the basket then give it to God.

Once I did this. I saw Him take the evil spirit out of the person. He did away with the spirit and the evil that was manifested by it. The fire of God burned it up. I was left in the scene with God's peace and goodness surrounding me. For the rest of my life, I did not have to bear the scene of evil, for God had written on my soul His beautiful will for me which was goodness and peace.

Our God is the Living God who is living in the past, the present, and the future. He wants to rewrite on your heart His will for your past if you will let go of it. (If you will not hold it as your identity and as that which shapes your future). Offer it to God and invite Him to come into it.

In your own journal or on the blank page write the scene or scenes which you would like Jesus or Father to come into and meet you there, the circumstances in your life which need to be redeemed. Write about any evil which you wish God to take from your heart, any mental images or symbols of evil which plague your mind.

# *My Journal*

## DATE:

*Scenes I would like Jesus or Father God to come into and meet me there.*

# CHAPTER 3

# Inner Healing Prayer: How Do I Pray It?

God your Father sent His Son Jesus to heal your heart. "…He has sent me to heal the brokenhearted…" (Luke 4:18, NKJV). In inner healing prayer you say come Lord Jesus or come Father God and heal my heart. Come into my moment of time when my heart was hurt, or when I needed you, or when I need you in the future, or come when I disobeyed you. Come Lord and show me why I am reacting in such a way or why this is so hard for me. As you close your eyes and quiet your mind, you are inviting God to let you see, hear, or feel Him through your spirit in a particular time frame of your life either of His choosing or your choosing. It can happen in the present moment, in a scene from the past, or a projected future scene of your life.

Holy Spirit can make Jesus or Father known to you in several ways. He does this by letting you see Jesus in your mind's eye, (some describe this as seeing with the eyes of your heart); or by feeling His Presence beside you, in front of you, behind you, or in you; by communicating to you what He is saying or doing; or by allowing you to see through His eyes or feel through His heart. "…the Spirit of truth…He shall testify of me" (John 15:26, NKJV). He communicates with some people through symbols which have a special meaning to them, and to others who see Him putting things together or taking things away in their lives like with a puzzle.

When I first learned about inner healing prayer, I felt there was something wrong with me because God didn't seem real to me in this kind of prayer as He did to others. They were seeing Jesus easily. When I prayed and tried to see Him, He wasn't real. Then I learned God created us differently in the way we perceive Him, and one way is not any better than another. The truth is He gave us all the ability to know Him, and when we seek Him in love and in faith, He makes Himself known in whatever way is real to us. "And he who loves Me shall be loved of My Father, and I will love him and manifest Myself to him" (John 14:21, NKJV).

With me, the Lord is most real when I feel His Presence rather than seeing. However, as I have practiced inner healing prayer over the years, I have grown in the ability to see with my heart (or spirit) as well as sometimes knowing what God is saying to me through symbols. And sometimes when I pray, it is with the Father and sometimes it is with Jesus.

It is the very Presence of God that heals your heart. In inner healing prayer you are giving God permission to be Lord of a time in your life which may have caused you pain, fear, sadness, conflict, shame, or a time of indecision; and to rewrite or write that time of your life according to His will. He rewrites or writes it according to the script of Heaven which is in His heart for you. In inner healing prayer you see former, present, or future situations and circumstances of your life from His perspective.

Only God knows the whole truth about your life for He is the Truth. Jesus said, "I am the way, the truth, and the life…"

(John 14:6). He understands why you did certain things and what was behind what happened to you, for He understands the hearts of people and the realities of the unseen spirit world. "For the Lord does not see as man sees; for man looks at the outward appearance, but the Lord looks at the heart" (1 Samuel 16:7, NKJV). Inner healing prayer is letting God show you what He knows and sees, through the eyes of your heart. In inner healing prayer God helps you understand why people in your life, or why you, acted in a certain way. This understanding does not excuse sin, but forgiveness and reconciliation, healing and wholeness begin to happen when you understand the "why."

He knows and understands your future. You can invite Him into your future and trust the directions in which He guides you. I was praying inner healing with one of my grandsons as to which college he should attend. We asked Holy Spirit to show him Jesus taking his hand and walking onto the campus of the right one. The Lord did that, and my grandson was relieved because the stress of the decision was taken away. He is now very happy at that college.

When we invite Jesus to be Lord of any situation of our life, He is able to come into that situation as we view it in our heart and to call into being those things which be not as though they were (Romans 4:17), and the things which are not, to bring to nothing things that are (I Corinthians 1:28). In other words, the Lord calls into being the good, the beautiful, and the holy in that situation of your life to bring to nothing the things that happened the first time. Earth's records are not changed, but He changes the history of your heart in Heaven's records for eternity.

When you are ready to pray inner healing prayer, sometimes it's best to invite Father or Jesus to share a happy or normal scene with you first, before going into a serious or scary scene. As you feel, see, or hear Him enjoying your happiness or a normal time with you, it will be easier to invite Him into a scene with fear or pain. It is necessary that you experience His goodness and love, knowing He is greater than all evil, and knowing He overcame our last enemy which is death. If the scene still seems too frightening, perhaps you have a friend that will come along side you and quietly pray and believe while God is healing your heart.

We need to quiet our souls from interrupting thoughts as we invite Holy Spirit to bring into focus the scene which we want God to heal. Sometimes we are surprised by the scene the Spirit chooses, it may be one that we've long forgotten. Sometimes our heart just hurts, and we don't know what needs to be healed. He knows because He loves you, and He's been there all the time. He will bring up a repressed memory that is pertinent to the healing of your heart when you are secure in His love.

Just trust Him to bring up the right scene. We then invite Jesus or Father to be Lord of that moment, "Behold, I will do a new thing..." (Isaiah 43:19). The darkness cannot hide from Him, the night shineth as the day (Psalms 139:12). He sets at liberty those who have been bruised (Luke 4:18), those whose hearts have been hurt.

If you have been involved with Satan's spirit world in the cults or occult, you must not pray inner healing prayer until these are renounced and forgiveness is received, even if the involvement was a long time ago. The influence of Satan's spirit world lingers, and God's Spirit will not mix with Satan's spirit. If this involvement is not renounced, you may experience Satan's evil manifestations or even sadness or fear when you attempt to have inner healing prayer.

This involvement would include the cults such as teachings that deny Jesus is the Son of God, that there are other ways to come to God besides through His Son, or that something more is required for our salvation other than His blood shed for our sins. Jesus said, "… I am the way, the truth, and the life: no man comes unto the Father, but by me" (John 14:6).

It would include the occult such as seeking extrasensory knowledge by ways other than our Lord (there are only two spirit worlds, one of God's Holy Spirit and the other, Satan's evil spirit world). Deuteronomy 18:10-11 tells us that these things are detestable to God, and He forbids them; fortune-telling, sorcery, interpreting omens or engaging in witchcraft, casting spells (hypnotism), functioning as a medium or psychic, or calling forth the spirits of the dead. Also, horoscopes, yoga (which is more than exercise, which includes chants to Hindu demon gods), any New Age practices, tapping which is seeking or guiding spiritual energy from the body, and recreational mind-altering drugs should be renounced as these can open the door to evil spirits.

As you renounce each activity that you were involved in as evil, naming them aloud with your voice and asking forgiveness through the blood of Jesus, God will cleanse you, setting your body and mind free of any wicked spirits and shutting the door to their influence. I've often explained it by saying, in the winter if your door is just cracked open a little bit, a cold draft comes in, but you don't realize where it's coming from. When the door is tightly shut, there is no draft.

If you have been heavily involved in these things, it would be best to seek deliverance by a known ministry of such. When you have finished renouncing all evil, asked forgiveness, and the spirits have been cast away, then the minister can pronounce that you are forgiven and cleansed (absolution).

If there is no minister to do this, you can pronounce over yourself that you have been forgiven and cleansed by saying these words from the Bible. This is speaking the Word of God, "If we confess our sins, He is faithful and just to forgive us our sins and to cleanse us from all unrighteousness" (1 John 1:9). When our spirit hears the Word of God, faith comes. "So then faith comes by hearing, and hearing by the word of God" (Romans 10:17). Also, if you are familiar with the practice of using Holy Water and have access to some, it is good to put it on your forehead with the sign of the cross proclaiming your cleansing.

After you have done these things, give your Father, God a period of time to clear your mind and body of evil thoughts, images, and feelings; and replace them with wholesome ones before you try to have inner healing prayer. Spend much time reading God's Word. His Word washes our minds, it is His love letter to us. Also spend time worshiping with fellow believers. If you try to have inner healing prayer too soon, you may find that evil thoughts and pictures are coming up when you want to pray.

As a child, I was involved with playing with a Ouija board at a Halloween party. Of course, I didn't know there was anything wrong in asking the Ouija board questions. As an adult, I learned that I was asking evil spirits, and I knew I should renounce that involvement and ask forgiveness, even though at the time I didn't know it was wrong. When we ask forgiveness for sins known and unknown at the time, both are put under Jesus's blood. This frees us from any evil influence, and the door is shut tight.

I became aware of another incident involving a woman and yoga. She was a Christian, and she thought it was alright to choose, like from a smorgasbord, the things she liked about yoga and also New Age thoughts and practices. For exercise, she had attended a course in yoga, and that teacher had not emphasized any of its spiritual roots from the Hindu religion. So, she signed up for another course. This teacher was different, she was involving the class in bowing to the demon Hindu gods with chants and prayers. The woman who was a Christian simply put her hands together and bowed saying, "Lord Holy Spirit, I bow to you and worship you."

At the next class time when she came to the studio, it was completely demolished! Shocked, she was told that a driver during the night had run into the shopping center demolishing the studio, not hurting the businesses on either side. The woman realized, if you are a Christian, you carry God's Spirit in your body, for your body is His temple, and He will not sanction where there is traffic in Satan's spirit world.

If you need to do the work of renouncing and asking forgiveness, write specifically each thing you were involved in, then with your voice renounce them one by one as evil and ask the Lord out loud to forgive you and to rid you of these things forever. God's power is manifest when we put voice to our words, and the door is shut tightly to Satan's influence. In exchange, then ask your Heavenly Father to fill you with His Holy Spirit.

This does not mean putting away close family members or loved ones in your life who may still be involved in wrong things. We are called by God to live in peace and love with one another as much as is possible, and to stand in faith praying for each other.

## *My Journal*

DATE:

*Things I am renouncing and asking forgiveness for, having to do with Satan's evil spirit world.*

You may not have been involved with the evil spirit world in the previous ways, but there may be oppressing spirits that have attached to the wounds in your heart. In this situation inner healing prayer and deliverance go together. Sometimes you may need one before or after the other. (I am speaking of deliverance from demonic oppression not demonic possession of which deliverance requires experienced ministry.) You will know if you are bothered by a spirit because it is like an animal that keeps nipping at your mind, your emotions, your body, or you may just feel "out of sorts" not knowing why.

As a Christian, you must discern and proclaim to yourself that these feelings and thoughts are not the real you, and they are not of God. God's Spirit within your spirit, which is your true self, is greater than any evil spirits. "…because greater is He that is in you, than he that is in the world." (1 John 4:4). That said, the need for forgiveness, deliverance, and your freedom is not lessened. By your will, through the power of God, they shall be cast out.

They could be of anger, fear, sadness, rejection, the victim mentality, or others. We can pray deliverance for ourselves or with a prayer partner according to James 4:7 which reads, "Submit yourselves therefore to God. Resist the devil, and he will flee from you."

When we submit ourselves to God, we are putting ourselves under our Heavenly Father, we are aligning our hearts with His loving nature and His Word, the Bible. We ask Him to forgive us for our thoughts, feelings, or actions that have been against His nature and His Word. We may also need to ask Him to forgive us for things we did when or after our hearts were hurt. He understands the "why" behind these things, and

He doesn't condemn us. But we must ask forgiveness, then He can clear our souls by Jesus's blood from Satan's camp.

We say with our will, we are not going to have anger, fear, sadness, rejection, the victim mentality, or anything else that is the enemy's scheme to destroy us. We ask God to forgive us for allowing any of these things in our life. We give ourselves as well as any other person His gift, the washing of our sins and their sins away.

We then resist the devil by calling the spirit or spirits by name aloud and saying, "On the authority of Jesus the Christ and His blood that was shed for my sin, I bind you and send you away from me back to Hell from where you came." Often times we feel the deliverance through the exhaling of our breath. We then ask Father to fill us with His Holy Spirit where those spirits were oppressing our minds, emotions, or bodies.

The devil has to flee, but he may try to come back later. If so, stand firm on the authority and name of Jesus. Remember Jesus is the Son of God and He said, "…nothing shall by any means hurt you" (Luke 10:19). "And the seventy returned again with joy, saying, Lord, even the devils are subject unto us through thy name" (Luke 10:17).

It is good to hold the palms of your hands up to Father to receive the gift He wants to give you in place of the spirit or spirits that were cast away. Listen for a word or a picture He will give you of your new gift. Often it is the opposite of the evil spirit, like joy for sadness. Write it in your journal.

# *My Journal*

## DATE:

*Persons I am forgiving.*
*Things and/or spirits which I am renouncing and casting out*
*and asking God to forgive me for allowing them in my life.*
*The gift God is giving me in place of the evil spirit.*

I am now ready to pray inner healing prayer.

*Do I need to invite Jesus or Father to come to a happy scene or a normal one before I ask Him to come to a difficult one?* Your Heavenly Father loves you, you're the only "you" He has, and He delights to be present with you. It is always good, for your sake to invite Him to share a happy or normal time, if you can think of one, before asking Him to come into a difficult or frightening memory.

*Do I need a person who believes in inner healing prayer to pray with me?* If you feel afraid to pray, ask Father to direct you to the right person to pray with you. And, if that person does not know about inner healing prayer, perhaps you can share what you have learned with them. They can come alongside you and quietly pray while you are experiencing the Lord. Sometimes, it is helpful for the one having inner healing to speak aloud and describe what he or she is experiencing. If you are praying alone, it is still helpful to describe by speaking aloud to God and to yourself what you see or feel is happening.

You can always abandon yourself to Father and say, "Come and heal my heart in whatever memory or time You choose." Remember He is longing to heal your heart. Some wounds in your heart can be healed in one prayer time, for others it will be a process of inner healing prayer and growing in your faith through the study of God's Word, the Bible and worshipping and serving with other believers.

As you become strong in faith practicing the Presence of the Lord, inner healing prayer will become a way of life, not only for times to heal your heart, but also for times of sharing the joyful and little moments of life with Him.

Write how you experienced Jesus or Father in the scene, what He told you or what you saw, how you felt in His love and Presence. Write about the healing of your heart. Do you need to pray more inner healing about this scene or situation? If so, as you journal each prayer time, each will build on the one before until you are secure in your healing, knowing God has done it.

## *My Journal*

### DATE:

*My inner healing and how my heart was healed.*

# CHAPTER 4

# Stories of Hearts Being Healed

## *An Amazing Inner Healing After Thirty Years*

I want to tell you about a woman's most amazing story of inner healing after thirty years. Growing up, she had an irrational fear and dislike of Asian people and did not want to have anything to do with the oriental culture. This was not a problem until as an adult, her husband wanted to adopt an Asian son. Just the thought of it was greatly disturbing and conversations about it would bring tears. But God unmistakably spoke to her and told her, he was to be her son and she was to be his mother! They adopted the son when he was a young child.

For the next ten years she felt like a wretch. She knew she was supposed to love her son and she wanted to love him, but her irrational fear and dislike of Asians was in the way. She went through all the rational reasonings as to the "why" of her problem. Such as, she grew up during World War II and the Japanese were enemies. Also, she heard her mother tell of visiting San Francisco in the 1930s and seeing opium addicts lying on the street in Chinatown. This was frightening to a child. But her rational reasons didn't change the problem. She prayed many times asking and crying out to God to change her feelings. Then a friend gave her a book[1] about prayer in a new way, inner healing prayer. What did change the problem was inner healing!

It happened at an inner healing conference in a hotel where several hundred people were attending. The speaker told the audience to ask God to bring to mind a scene which He needed to heal as they quieted themselves and closed their eyes. He brought to her mind a scene which she had long forgotten. She was ten years old standing by a campfire listening to a conversation by adults. A woman was describing in detail the horrors which her relative experienced while being tortured by Japanese soldiers in a prison camp. God told her that was where her fear and dislike of Asian people began because she had internalized this evil and was passing it on.

Evil is sticky, when we hear of it being done to others or when it's done to us, it sticks to us, and we want to pay it back. Thus, we become that which we hate. We pass on evil, and only the blood of Jesus and forgiveness can unglue us and set us free from it. From that day until the then present, the evil of those soldiers stood between her and every Asian person she had known, even her child.

In the inner healing prayer time, God showed her in her mind's eye faces of four Japanese soldiers and told her to forgive them. Her thoughts were, *how can I? I don't know if these men are still on earth or if they are in Heaven or Hell.* God let her know that this makes no difference. When the blood of His Son is offered for the forgiveness of sin, and you personally forgive them, it will not change their place, but they and you will be released from that particular bondage of evil. She did not try to understand this theologically, but she took Him at His word.

The conference had scheduled Holy Communion that evening. God told her that during the service to see the cross over the altar and His Son dying on the cross for what took place in the prison camp and for her own sin of internalizing the evil and passing it to the Asian race. In the service when the priest raised the chalice signifying the blood of Jesus for the forgiveness of sins, she spoke to each Japanese face and said, "I forgive you." Then she asked God to forgive her. This did it, God set her free! Suddenly she felt light and happy inside. Her heart was healed. What glorious happiness!

She couldn't wait for the conference to be over and to go home and love her son. That hug was different than all the years before! When her son was older, she asked him to forgive her.

The next week in a swimming pool where there were only a few people swimming, she found herself near the end of the pool alone with a Japanese man. Ordinarily she would have been afraid of him, her heart would have seen him as a symbol of evil, but God had done away with that symbol in her heart! Surprisingly, she found herself wishing she could speak to this stranger and say something that would bless him.

That day on the boardwalk she saw a Japanese family including tiny children as well as grandparents. How she wished she could hug each one! This was her real spirit person without the ugly lying symbol keeping her heart captive. Her heart was free to love Asians after over thirty years of bondage. It was exhilarating, she wanted to hug the whole world and tell them God is good!

When we have harmed another person or persons by our sin and God forgives us, does He leave that other person or persons injured for the rest of their lives? This was what she had to face with her child. "Would my sin with the Asian race and all its ramifications leave my son injured for life?" No, God is too loving, too good, and too all powerful for that to happen. What is impossible with men is possible with God (Matthew 19:26).

When we give anything to Jesus that is ours to give, and let go of it, even the effect of our sins on others, He can miraculously turn it into good, because He is the Redeemer. He paid for it all on the cross, both our sin and its effect, but we must receive what He paid for through faith with our prayers. It is good to make a basket with the palms of your hands and to put in the basket all of the hurt that you caused, and even with your tears, lift it up to Father, asking Him and trusting Him to take it and turn it into good for those you've hurt. Only God can do this.

This is illustrated so well in the story of Joseph in the book of Genesis. His older brothers were jealous of their father's love for Joseph. They sold him into slavery to some traders who were traveling to Egypt. The brothers dipped his tunic in blood showing it to their father who then assumed a wild animal had killed Joseph. God was with Joseph, and many years later he became second in command to Pharaoh because God gave him the interpretation to Pharaoh's dream concerning a future famine. Joseph wisely stored grain during the plentiful years so that when the famine came, he saved Egypt and the surrounding lands even his own brothers who had so mistreated him. Joseph said, "But as for you, you meant evil against me; but God meant it for good…" (Genesis 50:20).

We can, and must, pray inner healing prayer for persons we have hurt. You do not have to be present with other persons to pray inner healing for them. It is possible to ask Jesus to enter their history with you when you hurt them and to heal their hearts. It is a wonderful miracle of our Lord when we see Him taking our sin which caused the hurt and annihilating it and bringing His love, goodness, and redemption to others' lives where there was harm. The persons you have hurt do not need to know about your inner healing prayer for them in order for God to touch them for good.

Do you have a symbol in your heart about a race or nationality which is not true like the woman had? Of course, she knew with her rational mind that all Asian people were not evil and were not to be afraid of, but the lying symbol kept her heart captive.

If your story is like hers, write down on the blank page the race, nationality, or group of people that you cannot love because of a lying symbol. If you know you have hurt persons or groups because of the symbol, write their names so you can pray for them. God can and wants to take that symbol away and heal your heart as well as those you may have injured.

Ask Him where and how the seed was planted that caused the symbol to grow. Ask Jesus or Father to go back with you to the scene. What is He telling you or what is He doing about the situation? He will help you forgive persons, races, even nations, and yourself. As you do, speak the words aloud. If the symbol was birthed through fear or violence, let Jesus or Father hold you, comforting you in their great power and love. Where God's Presence is, there can be no fear, no evil because His power and love are greater. Write what God showed you, what He said or how you emotionally felt in His Presence and what your response was in the scene. If you have hurt others because of the lying symbol in your heart, ask Him to forgive you and see Jesus taking the hurt away from them.

## *My Journal*

DATE:

*The lying symbol and how it got birthed in me. What Father or Jesus did to set me free. How God forgave me and how He is taking the hurt away that I may have caused.*

_____
_____
_____
_____
_____
_____
_____
_____
_____
_____
_____
_____
_____
_____

# *The Woman Who Forgave Her Father*

This is the story of a woman who as a child had been the victim of sexual abuse from her father. She could not forgive him, and he ended up in a mental asylum with the loss of his mind. Some years later in a Christian church service the minister asked those that needed to forgive someone to come to the altar. She knelt there, asking God to give her the gift of forgiveness for her father. If you are not willing to forgive, God can make you willing, if you will ask Him. She forgave her father, releasing him from her anger and washing his sin away in the blood of Jesus.

Strangely enough, a call came from the asylum saying her father had regained his complete mental ability. She asked when it happened, it happened the very hour she was kneeling at the altar. Again, a call came sometime later, saying come for him, there is no need to keep him here any longer.

This illustrates the power of forgiveness in the unseen spirit world like the man I prayed with who forgave his father. "If you forgive the sins of any, they are forgiven them; if you retain the sins of any, they are retained" (John 20:23, NKJV). Jesus spoke these words after His resurrection when He gave the disciples the Holy Spirit to dwell within them, that same Spirit that resided in Him to forgive sins. It is an awesome thing that God has granted to us through the Holy Spirit, the power to forgive those who have wronged us, and forgiving them, we can set them free to know and love Him.

God is Love, He made us like Himself to love and to forgive. Jesus gave us the ultimate example of love and forgiveness when they nailed Him on the cross. He said, "Father, forgive them; for they know not what they do" (St. Luke 23:34). To live in unforgiveness is to give place for the devil to stand in our lives. When we forgive and are forgiven, he has no place to stand, he will fall.

Is there someone you need to forgive and release him or her from your anger? Maybe you are no longer angry with them, but the sin they committed against you still has them bound. Forgiving the sin doesn't mean you are denying that it happened or excusing it or justifying it, but you are simply believing the truth that Jesus took it into His own body and paid the price with His crucifixion for it to be forgiven. Forgive, so your own heart can be free from the bondage of the sin, and you will be setting the other person free to know God! Sin is like a double lock; it locks the hearts of both persons. When the victim forgives the perpetrator, the victim's heart is set free, and the perpetrator's heart is unlocked for God to come into.

In inner healing prayer ask Father or Jesus to be with you as you close your eyes and see with your heart the person in front of you that you want to forgive. Sometimes the sin against us has been so great that we can not look at the one who perpetrated it, but with our Father or Jesus there, standing beside us, it is possible to forgive.

## *My Journal*

DATE:

*Persons and sins I forgive.*

_____

_____

_____

Chapter 4

## *A Friend Facing Divorce*

This story is about a friend whose husband was divorcing her to marry another woman. Though he had been unfaithful in their marriage my friend was still in love with him and very much wanted to keep their marriage together. The divorce went through and on the day he was marrying the other, my friend asked me to pray with her. How could she go on in life with the agony of thinking about him being married to another when she still loved him? Her heart was hurting.

We quieted ourselves and asked God to come into that present moment and tell us His answer. He did. The Lord told her she did not have to throw her love for her husband away, like in the garbage can or under the rug, that she could give it to Him. All that was good, He would keep in His heart for her.

With the palms of her hands making a basket, she put into it all the happy and sweet moments she had experienced with her husband. There were moments at college dances, times with their children on family vacations, on their boat, and at their cabin. She put these moments and all of her love for him in the basket and lifted it up to God that He might put it into His heart. She let go of it as she gave it to God. Then she asked Father to cause her heart to forget how it loved her husband.

God is the only One that can cause your heart to forget how it has loved, and when He does, it's as if the heart never knew that person the same way. This is one of the most powerful prayers I know, one that must not be entered into lightly. Because, when He causes the heart to forget, it forgets and there is no more emotional bonding.

My friend's heart and life were healed. She went on to lead a very productive single life being a missionary for thirty-five years with no longing or sadness for her ex-husband. Although, she continued to pray for him and his two additional wives with great results. His relationship with their children changed for good and his third wife became a Christian minister.

Is there a relationship in your life that has ended or one that should end, and you cannot let it go? If there is an emotional hook in your heart with this person that is not good, God wants your heart to be free. Free to meet life afresh. Free to have new beginnings with no shadow over you of a lost love.

God will tell you if you need to pray the prayer to cause your heart to forget. If so, perhaps it will be easier for you to write on the page provided or in another journal the things in the relationship which were good, not sinful things, but things that were a blessing to you. God will hold in His heart anything righteous and good if we ask Him. With God nothing is lost because He is eternal. Think about these things as love gifts from your Father, and then put them in the palms of your hands and give them back to Him. Let go! Then ask Him to cause your heart to forget how it loved that person! The things you gave to your Father in Heaven will be in safe keeping in His heart for eternity time, but for earthly time, your heart will be free, free from bondage.

# My Journal

DATE:

*A relationship in which my heart needs to forget how it loved and how God caused it to forget.*

## *A Heart Who Loved Too Much*

One woman had to ask God to cause her heart to forget how she had loved her mother. She was in idolatry to her mother who had died, and the emotional hook in her heart was causing her to try to live out her mother's life instead of her own.

When we idolize another person, whether it be a family member, a spouse, a friend, or someone else, our emotions are tied to that one in a wrongful way. We are not free to be the person God created us to be. Our first love which should be His, has been given to another. When our first love is His, then we are safe to love others. We can't be caught in traps that ruin our life. God does not want His children's lives ruined by anyone or anything. Proverbs 4:23 tells us to "Keep thy heart with all diligence; for out of it are the issues of life."

This woman knew that idolatry was a grave sin, one that drew the strongest suffering in the Old Testament of the Bible. For God said we were to have no other gods before Him (Deuteronomy 5:7). Yet, everything good in this woman's life seemed to have come from her mother, even her love for God. It was hard for her, for it seemed as if she was turning her back on everything beautiful, everything true and real, and the sweetest love she had ever known.

We all come to that moment in life where we have to trust God's love for us more than anyone's. She did trust Him. She asked her Father God to forgive her for making her mother her idol, though she was afraid when she prayed the prayer for her heart to forget. She didn't know what to expect, and how it would change her feelings. God was faithful, her heart was free. He took away the emotional hook. The love for her mother was not on the front burner of her life 24/7, but it was back where it should be, in the memory albums of her heart. She was free to discover the person God created her to be and to begin the exciting new adventure of living her life rather than trying to live her mother's.

In this case idolatry happened because of loss of that which was good, and the fear of never being able to retain it. This woman's mother had poured into her the goodness of life. She was trying to retain that goodness and hold on to it through the idolization of her mother.

God made us to love that which is good in life, for all goodness comes from Him, everything precious, everything beautiful, everything real and true. But He made each of our hearts to know Him and receive fresh love from Him every day like an artesian well of water. If we set our hearts on or idolize the good which comes from Him, rather than the source Himself, our hearts are left in stagnant water. "…Jesus stood and cried out, saying, 'If anyone thirsts, let him come to Me and drink. He who believes in Me, as the Scripture has said, out of his heart will flow rivers of living water'" (John 7:37 – 38, NKJV).

Is there a person in your life or a thing that is your idol? Father tells us that we should love Him with all our heart, soul, mind, and strength (Deuteronomy 6:5). If He is our first love, then we are free to love others to our heart's content, for we will love them with the love of the Lord, and we will be safe.

Can you trust Him and His love for you? Can you believe that He loves you more than anyone else loves you? Draw near to Him, talk to Him. He will draw near to you (James 4:8). He loves you as if you were the only person in this world. He made you, you came from His love. He longs for your company, and when you talk to Him, He will give you His full attention.

Write what you'd like to say to God, then write what you feel He's saying to you. Each day in your "quiet time" with Him, journal your conversation. At the end of the day write the little ways or the big ways He's loved you or showed you His love.

## *My Journal*

### DATE:

*A person or thing in my life that has taken first place, God's place in my heart. I'm asking Him to forgive my idolatry and to cause my heart to forget how it loved that person or thing. What God told me and how He assured me of His love forever.*

_____

_____

_____

_____

_____

_____

_____

_____

_____

_____

_____

## *A Man Caught in the Trap of Adultery*

This man was grateful that God could and did cause his heart to forget how it loved the wrong person. He had been happily married for many years, but then a young woman came into his life. In some ways she made him feel better about himself than his wife did. He was greatly distraught. He did not want to divorce his wife and turn his back on their children and grandchildren, and yet the emotional hook was in his heart. He asked the Lord to forgive him. He asked the Lord to cause his heart to forget how he loved the other woman, and he meant it. God was faithful, his heart did forget, and the emotional bonding was broken. His wife forgave him, and his marriage was saved.

Are you caught in adultery? Do you want out of the trap? God will help you. If possible, kneel. Tell God you are sorry for breaking His commandment and hurting Him as well as your spouse. "If we confess our sins, he is faithful and just to forgive us our sins, and to cleanse us from all unrighteousness" (1 John 1:9). To repent when you ask forgiveness is to turn with your will and go in the opposite direction. But in order to do this, you must ask God to cause your heart, mind, and body to forget how you loved that other person. He will set you free. Let His great love for you sustain you. If you are still captive, you may need to pray deliverance from a spirit of lust.

# My Journal

DATE:

*My prayer asking God to cause my heart to forget how it loved a person or persons. My prayers of repentance and asking forgiveness. What God told me and how He set me free.*

## *The Woman Who Couldn't Forget Her Grandfather's Suicide*

This story is about a woman in her forties who came to me for prayer. She had been haunted for years by her grandfather's suicide. When she was ten, coming home from school one day, she found his dead body and the grisly details in their basement. Every week since then this memory would appear in her mind, she couldn't forget it, and she felt like her grandfather ruined her life.

It was too difficult for her to ask Jesus to come to the suicide scene, so we asked Him first to come into some happy times with her grandfather. It was amazing the scenes He brought to mind that she had forgotten. Satan always wants to block our memory of that which is good about a person by something bad which happened because of them or to them.

Jesus caused her to remember how her grandfather often met her walking home from school, how he had a pet nickname for her which she loved, and how she sat beside him when he played the piano. She remembered that one Easter he gave her a cross. These memories warmed her heart, and she said she saw him from the Lord's perspective when he was playing the piano. He was ill and suffering pain, something that as a ten-year-old she never knew. It was that which caused him to take his life.

After these happy prayer times with Jesus there, she was ready for Him to come with her to the suicide scene. But still afraid to go down in the dark basement where the grandfather's body lay, Jesus let her walk behind Him half hidden by His robe. As they went down the steps, suddenly she exclaimed, "The basement is no longer a dark and scary place, a place of death, it is full of light!" In the Bible, Jesus said, "I am the light of the world" (John 8:12). There can be no darkness where He is.

As they went toward the body, she stayed behind. Jesus did what He did in the city of Nain, when He raised up the young man who was dead on the bier (Luke 14 - 15). He raised the grandfather to a sitting position. Then the granddaughter heard him say with tears in his eyes, "Please forgive me." She came out from behind Jesus's robe and forgave her grandfather for all those years of haunting memories! That was all that was needed! The Lord's presence there and her forgiveness to her grandfather healed her heart! Leaving Jesus with the grandfather, she went out the basement door to a beautiful spring day to ride her bike and play as a ten-year-old.

I saw this woman about six months after the prayer, she told me, not once had the tormenting memories appeared since her heart was healed.

When we invite Jesus or Father God to come with us into our memories, He does a new thing! The emotional "hook" which keeps the heart captive is taken away. The old memory becomes dim, you can still remember it, but it has no emotional impact. The new memory with God is full of His light and love and truth.

Sometimes, the heart is healed with just one inner healing prayer, but other times inner healing takes place over a period of time. It is like installments, each prayer time with the Lord builds on the one before. That is why it is needful to journal.

Our enemy, the devil, would like for us to not remember our inner healing prayer times like dreams that disappear. When we write even the details of our experiences with the Lord, they become more vivid in our mind. God can and does often expand and interpret the experience as we journal it. Write the date on your journal page and how you experienced the Lord and the other persons in the scene. Then read your journal afresh before your next prayer time. It is a wonderful thing to go back later and read how God healed your heart and thank Him.

Do you have haunting memories from the past or phobias which you can't explain? Since the past is still available to God and He understands and loves your heart, ask Him to go with you to the scene or scenes where you became afraid. It could have happened when you were a very young child or even in the womb. Remember, He is all powerful, all good, and He loves you and knows every second of your life. The healing of your heart can begin today.

## *My Journal*

DATE:

*Memories where I was afraid,*
*and I ask God to come into them and heal my heart.*
*What Father or Jesus did to take away my fear.*
*How I felt His love and power overcoming all evil.*

_____

_____

_____

_____

_____

Chapter 4

# The Artist Who Couldn't Paint

This is a story about an artist who was in an invisible net. He found himself at a standstill, not being able to create, and he didn't know what was wrong. His heart wanted to create beautiful paintings, but he was stymied. Over a period of several prayer sessions, we discovered the "why."

His father, who also was an artist, developed heart disease. During the boy's growing up years, his father's heart caused the family many emergencies with 911 calls and hospitals. Their life revolved around the father's health issues, and the boy never had normal happy teenage years. His teenage-self developed a root of bitterness towards his father, and the symbol associated with him which of course was the father's creativity as an artist.

The son, an artist himself, was fighting against an invisible net which blocked his creativity. The father died, and the adult son realized that his father did not choose to have heart disease and to disrupt the family, but his teenaged-self needed to forgive his father and God for the circumstances of his young life.

In inner healing prayer, because God is outside of time, we can go back to any age to forgive someone even if that person has died. We can and should ask forgiveness for our self, even if we were a child and didn't realize our heart was holding a bitterness. It is necessary to see ourself as the child when we ask forgiveness and when we forgive a parent or some other person.

In prayer, the artist asked the Lord to forgive him for being bitter against his father. Then he asked the Lord to go back with him to his teenage-self. That teenager forgave his sick father and asked his father to forgive him. After doing this, he forgave himself, and the adult man gloriously found his freedom! Free from the hidden root of bitterness and the net, free to create to his heart's delight, so much so that soon he was showing his art in national galleries.

Many of us have invisible nets which we go through life fighting against. Our enemy, Satan, causes us to think we are incompetent or "second-grade" material which is not true. In actuality we are caught by a net through a symbol which our heart gave to a circumstance, a thing, or a person in our past life.

Symbols speak to the heart and the heart follows suit. Symbols keep the heart captive, they defy facts. If the symbol is birthed through what seems to be good to the heart, then the heart will follow it for good. If it was birthed through what was bad, the heart will follow it for ill. Only God can re-symbolize our hearts and remove labels, invisible labels that we find on ourselves or things or people that are not right and cause us to have nets. God is Love and He is Truth, and He makes things right and truthful, and He sets us free.

If lying labels attach to our hearts when we are children, we are not capable of reasoning or understanding the circumstances or a right response. In inner healing God gives us His understanding and a "second chance" to make the right response, often with forgiveness. The artist as a teenager couldn't make the right response to his father's illness. As a result, he had a root of bitterness towards his father and a wrong symbol connected to his father's creativity, or art.

The net comes because of sin, but God forgives sin. He forgives us as we forgive the circumstances or persons, and the symbol is made right, we are free of the net! We find we are capable of winning over that which was our nemesis. When sin can no longer hold us captive, we can live the way God intended, the right way in righteousness.

Has Satan put a symbol or label in your heart on circumstances or on people by their gender, by their race, by their nationality, which causes you to dislike or even hate, to be afraid of, or avoid them? Remember the woman with Asian people? He puts bad labels on that which God intends for good. Satan can also put a "too good" label in our heart for that which causes a net of self-indulgence or idolatry.

In the case of a circumstance, I knew of a little girl who had the unhappy experience of witnessing a fight in a public place. It was loud, and there were no police nearby to break it up. After that, she did not want to go to public places. She did not want to go shopping, even to grocery stores. Unknowingly, her heart had placed an unsafe label on these places through the circumstance of the fight, and thus the net came.

Some years later, though I was not present with her, I asked Jesus to go back to that scene and minister to the little child so as a youth she would not feel uncomfortable in public. Much to my surprise, as I was praying inner healing for her, and seeing with God, Jesus stopped the fight and ministered justice and then love to those fighting, rather than ministering to the child. All the while, the little girl in the scene was witnessing Jesus doing what no man did or could do.

In inner healing prayer we have a saying, "No man works like Jesus." We never know what He is going to do, but He is God, and He is the Redeemer, redeeming in our heart that which we have seen or participated in which was evil. That's how hearts are healed and there is no distance between Holy Spirit and the souls and spirits of people.

Jesus did bring healing to the girl's heart, and she was able more and more to go into public places although she never knew I prayed inner healing prayer for her. This may seem strange to you but think of it like bearing one another's burdens. "Bear one another's burdens, and so fulfill the law of Christ" (Galatians 6:2, NKJV). To fulfill the law of Christ, Jesus told us to love one another as He loves us. So, whether we are praying inner healing prayer or another type of prayer, as we are asking Jesus to bless that person, we are loving them with the love of God.

We can pray inner healing prayers for others even if they are not present with us. Some we may know, others we may not know, but Holy Spirit may tell us to pray for them by letting us know their need. We then ask Jesus or Father to go with them into scenes of their lives and bring forth His healing redeeming love. By faith we are giving our Lord Holy Spirit the opportunity to heal what has gone wrong in their lives. By faith we are opening a portal by which Holy Spirit can minister to a person's soul. We are seeing with God and acknowledging His healing redeeming love in that person's life. They need not ever know we prayed for them.

In the case of a "too good" label, our hearts can become captive in obsessive time spent. The thing or person labeled "good" by the heart becomes like a god to us in idolatry. The symbol is keeping the heart captive and defying facts thus we find ourselves in an invisible net.

With the "bad" label we may know that our feelings or actions are unreasonable and wish to be free of them, but with the "too good" label, our heart is caught in a web of "love" which we ferociously guard. We reason that "love" is good. We don't realize we're in a net because this person or thing which we idolize makes us "too happy" to be bad.

To cry out to be free from this net, takes either God's strong conviction or else the object of our love threatens us in some way or is taken from us. For the heart to be healed and truly free, we must with our will make Father God our first love and let Him re-symbolize our heart by both His written Word, the Bible and His rhema word spoken to us, as well as inner healing prayer.

If you have been in idolatry, take time to emotionally bond with Father, He wants to bond with you in your heart. He is really in love with you, and He knows and wants what's best for you. His love is the safe love because He is absolutely trustworthy. He is the One who can free you from the net and set love in order. Talk to Him. He's right there beside you. Write notes or letters to Him, and each day read the Gospel of John in the Bible. He will speak to you through His Word, the Bible. God, your Father created you to be free, not to be emotionally dependent on any person, substance, or thing except Him. He loves you more than anyone could ever love you.

On the page provided or in another journal, write about any invisible net which has kept you captive. Is it a negative net like the one the artist had, linked to a root of bitterness toward a person? Is it a negative symbol having to do with gender or race?

Is it a "too good" net which steals your time and steals your heart in self-indulgence such as a hobby, a sport, social media, even food, or is it the sin of idolatry of a person which keeps your heart from loving God, your first love? It could be a symbol which you've pegged your self-worth and identity to, thus holding your heart to something or someone which

God does not intend. If your parents or others praised you for something you did or something they wanted you to do, it may have become a symbol in your heart of your self-worth, which you have clung to with great tenacity. Thus, you find yourself in the net of always doing that, but never succeeding in what God purposed and planned for you. God made you for Himself not for any others, so your heart is safe when it holds no other symbol or label of self-worth except the exalted one, "I am a child of God"!

Is it a net that is keeping you from your full potential because some authority figure put a label on you? Maybe a parent, a teacher, a coach, an older sibling, or even a friend said you would never be able to do something, so you have an invisible label and net of being dumb, clumsy, slow, too fat, too short, or never good enough. Sometimes when we have become the victim of abuse whether it's verbal, emotional, or physical, we unintentionally take on the label of a victim. Then our heart causes it to play out in the different areas of our life. This is an insidious and deadly net because it blocks us from achieving the success that our Father God intends for us. We must in inner healing prayer ask Holy Spirit to go back to the scene or the repeated scenes whereby we were a victim and show us Jesus becoming that victim for us. He will do it, and He has made you more than a conqueror through Jesus who loves you (Romans 8:37). He has given to all of us His divine masculine will to accomplish all that we need to do and to become the head and not the tail (Deuteronomy 28:13).

Sometimes, women especially, if they have been abused as young girls will have a label on their back, invisible but nevertheless there, "Abuse Me." Even though they do not wish to be abused, they draw abuse. In this case it is best to have a prayer partner physically take the invisible label off and proclaim by God's Word, "If the Son therefore shall make you free, you shall be free indeed" (John 8:36). If you do not have a prayer partner, take hold of God's Word, by quoting it aloud and proclaiming your freedom. If you have accepted Jesus as your Savior, you are a new creation, no longer the abused one. God has given you His label, "My Innocent and Beautiful Child."

In quietness of mind, ask your heavenly Father to bring into focus the scene or scenes whereby the lying label was attached, or the symbol was birthed. Ask the Lord to come with you into the scene. I don't know what He will say or what He will do, but I know it will be good for He is your true Love whom you can always trust (1 John 4:16). He might take you in His arms and hold you to His breast and tell you, you are safe in His love.

He is the Truth (John 14:6). He is the One who re-symbolizes our heart and takes off the old label. You might see Him burning it up or destroying it in some way. He will give you His new label. Often it is the opposite of the old one. Listen for it and be sure to journal it.

Ask God to forgive you of any wrong choice you made even if you were very young and didn't know the choice was wrong. Ask Him to forgive you for believing the lying label and to forgive the person or others in the scene which caused you to have the label or caused your heart to birth the symbol. You may find yourself free of the net right away or you may need to allow Jesus or Father to go with you into more scenes. Make time for inner healing where Father or Lord Jesus can emotionally bond with your heart in love. He will complete that good work in you which He has begun, (Philippians1:6) for He loves you and longs to heal your heart and set you free of nets. You are His beloved treasure.

## *My Journal*

DATE:

*Scenes that have to do with my net or nets, and how Father or Jesus set me free. How He made new symbols for my heart. The new label that God gave me for myself, and the new labels He gave me for persons, circumstances, or things.*

_____

_____

_____

_____

_____

_____

_____

_____

_____

_____

_____

_____

_____

_____

_____

## *A Lady Who Couldn't Face Authority*

This story is about a heart which was in much need of inner healing and also deliverance from the oppression of evil spirits. It is about a woman who for most of her life had difficulty with bosses. Her authority issues stemmed from the transference of the symbol of her father to bosses. This symbol, which was born of his rage and misuse of authority had caused her rebellion, hate, and fear of authority figures.

Jesus showed her the truth behind the truth of her father's behavior, that as a little boy he too had been the victim of rage from a father. But in her heart, this did not excuse his sin of misusing his authority nor did it erase the symbol. She knew that in order for God to forgive her of her sin, she must forgive her father (Matthew 6:14,15). She wanted to want to forgive him, but God had to do something more in her heart.

God has given us His power to forgive. After His resurrection, Jesus breathed the Holy Spirit into His disciples, and said, "If you forgive the sins of any, they are forgiven them; if you retain the sins of any, they are retained" (John 20:23, NKJV). When we forgive someone, we are saying, "I no longer charge you or hold your sin against you, I am erasing it in my heart and asking God to erase it in His memory." "For I will forgive their iniquity, I will remember their sin no more" (Jeremiah 31:34). This opens up the pipelines between that person and God and that person and yourself. The sin which clogged the pipelines has been cleared away. Good things can begin to happen to both yourself and that person because you have forgiven them.

When Jesus was on earth, the people were incredulous that He could forgive sin, they believed only God had the power to forgive. Now, shockingly, Jesus has given us as Christians, through the Holy Spirit that dwells within us, that same power to forgive.

The oppression of evil spirits kept the woman from being able to forgive. Though she wanted to forgive her father, and she would say the words of forgiveness, but her heart was not changed. When a boss would ask her to do something in an authoritative tone, for hours and sometime days afterward, she would have thoughts of hatred and anger toward that one. She knew that these were unreasonable thoughts and that evil spirits were causing them. She realized she needed deliverance.

This woman had allowed fear, rebellion, and hate to fester in her heart. When this happens, it is like a wound not cared for. Evil spirits find a nest, and the person needs deliverance from demonic oppression as well as inner healing. (This is not demonic possession). Some persons need inner healing first and others need deliverance first. God will let you know.

The Bible tells us how to be delivered of the devil, "Submit yourselves therefore to God. Resist the devil, and he will flee from you" (James 4:7). To submit to God is to agree with Him, agree that He is right and you have been wrong, and to put yourself under His authority and ask forgiveness for anything in your life that's been out of line with His Word, the Bible. To submit is also to repent of where you have broken God's law (His heart) and to decide with God's help you are going to live right.

When we resist the devil, we define where he has attacked us and where his nest is. And if we are a Christian, we must also define that our real self is the self that is joined to God's Spirit, our spirit person (1Corinthians 6:17). We proclaim, (it is best to do this aloud) that we are a child of God who has been delivered from the power of darkness and has been translated into the kingdom of His dear Son (Colossians 1:13). We proclaim that He, the Holy Spirit, who is in us, is greater than he, the devil, who is in the world (1 John 4:4).

The devil cannot stand where the truth and the blood of Jesus is proclaimed and believed. His nest is washed out. He operates through lies. Jesus's shed blood on the cross won our forgiveness and defeated the devil, he has to flee. He may try to come back, but you proclaim that you are free. "…they overcame him (the devil) by the blood of the Lamb (Jesus) and the word of their testimony" (Revelation 12:11). "If the Son therefore shall make you free, you shall be free indeed" (John 8:36).

If this is you, write on the blank page what you need deliverance from, ask God for forgiveness and follow James 4:7. Describe your experience.

## *My Journal*

DATE:

*My deliverance.*

_____

_____

_____

_____

_____

_____

_____

You are under new authority, under new management, the management of God. If old habits pop up, just ask God for forgiveness and ask Him for His help in living the new life. Write down the practical help He gives you. "Faithful is He that called you, who also will do it." (1 Thessalonians 5:24). Trust God to do for you what you cannot do for yourself.

In inner healing prayer God showed this woman her father's real self, his spirit person. He was a Christian, so his spirit was joined to God's Spirit, but his soul had been damaged by his life's circumstances. Seeing his spirit person made all the difference. God gave to her what she had longed for all her life, to have a strong, kind, good father. He gave her back what she felt she had been cheated of. This sense of knowing her father's real self was like an anchor in her soul. Whenever his behavior or a memory of his behavior triggered old reactions, her anchor was her hold.

If you have had a similar problem with a person in your life, make time for inner healing prayer and ask God to show you the real person behind the behavior, the person God intends that one to be. Through inner healing prayer God pulls the curtain back on our earthly life and time zone and shows us eternity. We see the person God intended when that one was in the womb of His heart before he or she was born, not the one that has been damaged by life's circumstances. Remember, God can and does call those things which be not as though they were (Romans 4:17). When He shows you the real, write what you see and take hold of the real person in your heart, emotionally bond with that one. Then you will have an anchor when the seas are rough.

God sees that one in His Son Jesus, made new and whole and filled with His Spirit. To see with God is to pray. To see with God is faith, faith that causes His will to happen on earth as it is in Heaven. "… but faith which works by love" (Galatians 5:6). One must be in love with God to see as He sees. Faith becomes fun because God has plenty of faith for everyone. As you collaborate with Father and put your measure of faith from your heart, your mustard seed of faith with His great faith, great things will happen (Mathew 17:20). Jesus came not into the world to condemn us but to save us (John 3:17).

An amazing thing happened in this woman's life. After she had been delivered of the evil spirits, and was able to forgive her father, with a real heart change, and had received forgiveness for herself, she felt to forgive her current boss. The very next day her boss was a different person! All the old coldness was gone. It was like sunshine had happened between her and the boss. The pipelines between her and God and between her boss and God were opened because the blood of Jesus had cleared the way. Now there was no longer an unseen evil force between the boss and this woman.

We've been given an awesome privilege as Christians to be forgiven, to forgive others, and to even forgive ourselves through the blood of Jesus and the power of the Holy Spirit who dwells within us. This can change the world!

Are there people in your life who are sometimes unbearable, maybe a wife or a husband, a child, a friend, or a boss? Write that person's name in your journal. In a quiet time and space ask God to show you that person's real self. The real self is the one God planned when he or she was in the womb of His heart. When He shows you the person He planned, write what they are like and how you emotionally felt in their presence.

God does the work of transforming that person. You just have to be in agreement with Him that He wants to do it and that He will do it. Ask Him to give you His love for that one. Then you proclaim with words out loud that they are indeed the way God showed you. This is inner healing prayer, to see as God sees and with your words to proclaim that it is so. Remember, God is always good, He wants to forgive and change people, and Jesus made it possible for us all to be changed when He died for us on the cross. You have the awesome privilege of collaborating with Him by forgiving their sins against you, opening up the pipeline between God and them, and seeing and proclaiming their transformation in Christ as reality now.

## *My Journal*

DATE:

*The person I choose to forgive and to see their real self.*
*What is their real self like?*
*What I felt when I received God's love for him or her.*

_____

_____

_____

_____

_____

_____

_____

In my own life, God told me that he was setting me free to respond to people the way He intended them and not the way I was experiencing them. He also told me to say under my breath whenever I was around a person I didn't like, or a person who was giving me a hard time, "(Name) I love you." It's amazing when you say this even though you're not feeling it, the other person begins to change and soon there truly is love, God's love between the two of you. His love changes the world!

He knew us all before He formed us in our mother's womb (Jeremiah 1:6). His plan for us was for good, but we are all broken in some ways. He is the Ultimate Redeemer and Restorer of that which is broken.

## *A Man Who Was Not Ready for His Heart to Be Healed*

In this story the man's heart was terrified, but he was not ready for his heart to be healed. He was born in a family who were psychics, having the ability of extrasensory perception. He grew up as a child with this ability, not knowing that it was of Satan, not of God. When he became an adult, he frequently saw ghosts. Some of these spirits were ones he considered "good" others were angry, dark, and fearsome. His heart was terrified of these.

He was introduced to a minister who told him the truth that his ability was not of God, and that he (the minister) would pray deliverance for him to be free of the ability to see ghosts. The man would no longer have extrasensory perception, be able to read minds, and his heart would no longer have to be afraid.

Having not known God as his loving Father, this man could not trust God's goodness. He did not want to give up the ability of extrasensory perception, even though it was demonic. He felt that being able to read minds helped him "get through" life.

When we align our hearts with God, we do not have to be afraid of Satan's power. For Jesus said after He was raised from the dead, "…All power has been given to me in Heaven and on earth" (Matthew 28:18). Earlier, He told His disciples, "Behold, I give you power… and nothing shall by any means hurt you" (Luke 10:19).

It's not that God was condemning this man. He was a child and grew up not knowing that there are two spirit worlds and that we must not traffic in Satan's world (Deuteronomy 18:10-

12, Acts 16:16-18). But when we learn the truth, then we must agree with God and His Word, so that He can heal our hearts. This man was not ready for his heart to be healed.

Is there something in your life that you feel helps you "get through" yet you know it's not of God? It could be drugs, alcohol, indulgence in food, or something else? Can you trust His love, His goodness, and His ever present Being to help you "get through" without the dependence on that something else? Write the name of that "thing," and then tell God you want to trust Him. Ask Him for help and then let Him show you yourself without that "thing" in your life. You are complete in Him. "For in Him dwells all the fulness of the Godhead bodily. And you are complete in Him …" (Colossians 2:9-10). Write how you see Jesus or Father loving you and taking the place of the "thing," or taking it away.

## *My Journal*

DATE:

*The "thing" which helps me get through life is _____.*
*I give that "thing" to Jesus, and I take hold of Him instead.*
*Make a basket out of the palms of your hands and put that*
*"thing" in it, then hold it up and give it to God. I ask You,*
*God, to forgive me for depending upon it rather than on You.*
*I see my new life now without it, and Jesus is setting me free.*
*I proclaim I am complete in You.*

_____

_____

_____

# *The Man Who Was Ashamed of His Ethnicity*

This man had been ashamed all his life of his ethnic background. He had been born in the United States, but his family had all the characteristics of their former country. These characteristics were the butt of jokes as is the case with many countries. But to this man it was not funny, it was painful. Even though great artists and musicians had come from his ethnic background, he was not proud he came from the same stock. He wished he were someone else.

We can wish we were someone else for many reasons, maybe because of the character of our family, their lack of education, their lack of money, their lack of morals, or most of all because of the way they have treated us. If you wish you were someone else, God wants to heal your heart.

This man's heart got healed when he prayed inner healing prayer. Jesus showed him his family heritage redeemed, as he was willing to offer it to God, both his physical and environmental heritage. But first let's look at who we really belong to and what our real identity is.

God used humans to bring you forth to this world and you do bear in your body their physical characteristics, but your real identity comes from God. We belonged to God before we belonged to our family. He knew us before our family knew us. He loved us and chose us as His own and planned our place on earth before we were born (Jeremiah 1:5). We came from God and when we die, our spirit will return to Him. "Then shall the dust return to the earth as it was: and the spirit shall return unto God who gave it" (Ecclesiastes 12:7).

When we accepted Jesus as our Savior and Lord, God's Spirit entered into our spirit and we became identified with God in the most intimate way, being conceived anew as His child. With God's Spirit in our body, He identifies us with Jesus, "For we are members of His body of His flesh, and of His bones" (Ephesians 5:30). So, though we may look like our natural parents, in truth we have the spiritual DNA of our Father in Heaven. That being said, Father still wants us to love and not be ashamed of our earthly family.

In praying about your family heritage, you say, "Come Lord Jesus and be with me as you show me those whose genes you used to make up my body, mind, and emotions. Show me also those who have been an influence in my environmental heritage." You might see a room or a church with an aisle down the middle. Seated on one side, the ancestors of your father and on the other, those of your mother. (If there are family pictures, it would be helpful to look at them before praying.)

Some of these persons, you probably know very well including your mother and father, others you may only know a name or picture. You will have very definite feelings, perhaps some good some bad about those you know, but now you are asking Jesus to be in charge. You are asking Him to let you see the person behind the brokenness that you experienced or heard about. You are asking Him to show you the magnificence, the wonder, the beauty of some of the genes where talents could never flourish, and gifts were never nurtured. Jesus knows all things about these persons, about their lives. There may be aunts, uncles, cousins, or other extended family members who influenced your life.

Starting on one side think of the oldest person you know about or can remember, then with Jesus go to each one until you have prayed for all on both sides. Let Jesus tell you about each person, His love for them, the struggles they've had in life, their good or bad choices, or the good they accomplished. As always in inner healing prayer you may see pictures, have thoughts, words, or feelings come to mind; but Jesus's communication with you will always be in accordance with God's nature and His Word, the Bible.

If one exhibited evil or if you suffered evil from one, let Jesus deal with that. You will see Him destroy the evil in some way, and you will be comforted for that is His will. Then ask Him to sanctify or make holy the genes you received from that person or their environmental influence on your life. God can call those things which be not as though they were, and He has chosen the things which are not to bring to nothing things that are (Romans 4:17 and 1 Corinthians 1:28).

Just as Jesus took the little boy's lunch and lifted it up for His Father's blessing then received it multiplied to feed the five thousand, as you are willing to give to Him your family heritage, genes and all, you will see Him lift up for Father's blessing that which you have received. He makes it a holy gift to you from Him through every person. As you go from each one, thank Father for making that one's contribution to you holy. Then if you are able, thank Him for that person's life. If they are not living, you can ask Jesus to thank that one for you wherever they are.

It will take time to pray this inner healing prayer for all the ancestors you know down to your mother and father. You may need to pray it in several sessions.

If you come to persons that are difficult for you to forgive, ask Jesus to forgive them and then give you His gift of forgiveness for you to give them. This reminds me of my daddy giving me a quarter when I was a little girl to put in the offering plate in church. I didn't have any money to give, but my daddy had plenty of money to give, and he gave it to me to give. Your Abba, your Daddy God in Heaven has plenty of forgiveness to give, because Jesus paid for it all on the cross. Let Him give it to you to give.

After praying about your family heritage, and seeing or feeling Jesus make it holy, you can be proud of who God has called you to be on this earth. You may discover some dormant gifts hidden within you which Father God is going to bring forth and cause to flourish. He has given you your spiritual heritage, which is the same as His Son, and now He has made holy and blessed your earthly heritage!

## *My Journal*

### DATE:

*What Jesus told me and what He did*
*as I prayed the family heritage prayer.*
*How I felt and what I learned about different ancestors.*
*How Jesus healed my heart about my earthly heritage.*

_____

_____

_____

_____

_____

# CHAPTER 5

# Inner Healing Prayer and Your Body

God has created us as a trinity. We have a spirit (as God is a spirit), we have a soul (a mind, a will, and emotions) that expresses itself in this outward world through a body. In this chapter we will study what the Bible says about our body. We will address heart issues that relate to our body and the inner healing that is needed.

Let's see what God says about our body. "God said, let us make man in our image after our likeness: …So God created man in His own image, in the image of God created He him; male and female created He them" (Genesis 1:26–27). God created you, your body, your soul, and your spirit in His own image, like Himself and for Himself. God loves your body. Did you ever think about Him loving your eyes and nose, your fingers, and toes? Just as parents adore their babies' bodies so God adores our bodies. We are His babies. Of all of creation, we are the only creatures made in His image.

Maybe you are one who has had an abortion, and you deeply regret the killing of your baby's body. If this is the case, God is ready to forgive you and heal you. Yes, you destroyed His image, the person He knew and loved in your womb. "Before I formed you in the womb, I knew you…" (Jeremiah 1:5,

NKJV). But Jesus's blood covers your sin. He is longing to forgive you and heal your heart in inner healing prayer. And when He does, you must forgive yourself.

The following paragraphs could also apply to those who have had a miscarriage.

Jesus wants you to give your baby to Him. Luke 18:15-16 (NKJV) says, "Then they also brought infants to Him that He might touch them… Jesus called them to Him and said, Let the little children come to Me, and do not forbid them; for of such is the kingdom of God." He called mothers to bring their babies to Him, and He said of such is in Heaven.

Go back to that day of the abortion or the miscarriage. Your baby is yours. He or she does not belong to anyone else. No one can take that little one, you alone have the right to give him or her to God. As you close your eyes, ask Holy Spirit to let you see or feel Jesus there. When He is there, put your baby in the palms of your hands and then give your baby to Jesus. Say, "Lord Jesus, take good care of my baby in Heaven until I come, and tell my baby I love him or her." If you have had an abortion, ask Him to forgive you and ask your baby to forgive you. Say whatever your heart is yearning to say to that little one. Open the flood gates of your heart. Listen to what Jesus wants to tell you and write what He says. If you had an abortion, let yourself feel the forgiveness that Jesus is giving you, and then say aloud "I forgive myself," or even say your name.

He will love and take good care of your little one, and some day you will be reunited with your child in Heaven. Sometimes in inner healing prayer you will know what name your baby is to have. If so, you can name your child. Write all of this in your journal or on the blank page.

# *My Journal*

## DATE:

*Giving my baby to God, and if I had an abortion, asking God and my baby to forgive me, and forgiving myself. What I felt and saw and what Jesus told me.*

The Bible tells us that our body belongs to God that we are not our own. 1 Corinthians 6:19 (NKJV) says, "…do you not know that your body is the temple of the Holy Spirit who is in you, whom you have from God, and you are not your own?" Your body was made as a dwelling place for God! This is truly a "game changer!" My body is not my own! To think about my body as not belonging to myself changes all my thoughts about me, my face, my size, my mind, my physical abilities, etc. It is a freeing thought to think about your body belonging to God.

He has given me my body as a gift to live in while I am on earth. This causes me to want to be a good steward of my body for God. It causes me to want to treat my body with care and respect as I would want to take care of someone else's property.

A temple or a church is a place of worship, it is a beautiful place, a place of honor. Our bodies are beautiful to God, they represent a part of His image as does our soul and spirit. Our bodies are His place of honor, they are His dwelling place where He lives with us in our spirit.

Our bodies were bought back from Satan's dominion by the precious blood of Jesus. "For you are bought with a price: therefore, glorify God in your body, and in your spirit, which are of God's" (1 Corinthians 6:20). The price that God paid for us was the body, the flesh and blood of His Son. The crucifixion of Jesus was our ransom money. "Who gave Himself a ransom for all…" (1 Timothy 2:6).

Your body was bought with the most expensive price in the world, the life of God's dear Son. Thus, your body is of more worth and value than any material thing in the world. You are more precious, of more worth than can be measured by earthly standards. Just as you would treat and take care of your most valuable possession, so God wants us to treat and take care of our body which really belongs to Him.

The Bible says your body was made for the Lord and the Lord is for your body, He is not against it. He loves your body as well as your soul and spirit. This is counter to the religions that say the body is essentially evil. "Now the body is not for sexual immorality, but for the Lord, and the Lord for the body" (1 Corinthians 6:13, NKJV).

Are you a person whose heart is hurting because your body has been misused by someone else or by you. Your Father God has good news for you. He can heal your heart and forgive the misuse. In inner healing prayer He will come in, and His light and love will wash away all harm and hurt caused by someone or by you. Your body will feel new and clean again. He makes all things new and beautiful, and He will make you pure and innocent. For Jesus was innocent until He took up our sin and the sins done against us so that we could know innocence and be innocent again.

If you have been a victim of rape, incest or incest as a child, sexual slavery, or any sexual violation, you are probably very angry and justifiably so. Your heart is probably very grieved at having been violated. In the introduction to this book, I quoted Psalms 34:18 (NIV), "The Lord is close to the brokenhearted and saves those who are crushed in spirit." The sins which crush our spirits most and cause our heart to ache are those where we have been sexually violated, or where the intimacy in our marriage has been betrayed by a spouse. You have God's promise that He is close to you and that He will save (make well) your crushed spirit.

Once I had a brief time to counsel a young woman at a conference on inner healing. She was filled with anger for she had been a victim of incest repeatedly as a child. Her anger was turned toward God, and with fierce words she said, "Where was God when this was happening?" I said, "I don't know, but why don't you ask Him?"

She was quiet for a few moments, her anger subsided, and she closed her eyes. I knew God was very close. Another few moments passed, and a tear slowly rolled down her cheek. She said, "I saw Him on the cross. He was taking the abuse into His own body. That's where He was." He took it, she no longer had to bear the shame, He gave her back her innocence. 1 Peter 2:24 says, "Who His own self bare our sins in His own body on the tree…", the sins others have committed against us and the sins we have committed.

I left her in peace, God's peace that passes all understanding. In those moments He gave her that which I could not have given her with a lifetime of counseling words. He gave her Himself. He took into Himself the sin that had defiled her, He took it away forever, and she discovered herself a clean and beautiful new person in Christ Jesus.

If you have been the victim of rape, incest, or any sexual violation take these moments of quiet and ask God to heal your heart. Close your eyes and invite Him to come into your past when you were the victim or into the present moment. In His Presence no evil can happen. I don't know what He will do or what He will say, but I know He will bring healing. Wait and watch what He will do.

Let Him gather you in His arms and carry you in His bosom (Isaiah 40:11). Jesus bore in His own body on the cross that very sin that was done against you. You might see it being taken away by the wind or fire of Holy Spirit or dissolved and washed away by Jesus's blood. His love will make you whole again.

If you can, ask God to forgive your abuser so he or she will not burn eternally in Hell. That's a very long time for punishment and there's no exit. If you cannot forgive, ask God to help you to want to forgive and to so give you His mercy and love for that one that you'll be able to forgive in the future. Write how you felt God's Presence, what Jesus did or communicated to you, and how He healed your heart. Thank Him for His love.

## *My Journal*

DATE:

*Inviting Jesus or Father to heal my heart of sexual abuse. How I experienced the Lord.*

_____

_____

_____

_____

_____

_____

_____

_____

_____

Perhaps you were not the victim but the perpetrator of such sexual sins. Even if you only once violated someone sexually or if you were a partner in a mutual agreement of sexual sin, this is still very serious to God. He wants to forgive you and to cleanse you with Jesus's blood. Ask Him to forgive you and tell Him if you could have that time again, you would not break His heart and His commandment. Ask Him to heal the person you were involved with.

If through pornography, you betrayed your spouse and the intimacy of your marriage through illusory sex, this is the same as physical contact. For God tells us in Matthew 5:28, if we look with the eyes and lust, we have committed the act in our heart.

Pornography takes one deeper into sin, for it causes one to violate the image of God, for we were created in His image. It reduces His creation (woman or man) simply into sexual parts for one's own depraved use. This is a violation of God, Himself as well as a violation of His creation of the physical union for marriage. This union calls forth the oneness and intimacy in love that He has for each one of us, His children, like nothing else in creation (Ephesians 5:30-31). Pornography assaults this oneness and intimacy by defiling the very creation of our sexual being, and if one is married, by bringing into the marriage bed many others through illusory sex. But praise God, you can be delivered and freed from pornography and forgiven for all sin, for sin has to stop at the cross.

No matter what kind of sexual sin you are guilty of, Jesus had to become your sin, the very sin you did. "For He made Him who knew no sin to be sin for us, that we might become the righteousness of God in Him" (2 Corinthians 5:21, NKJV). Jesus had to pay the terrible price for our forgiveness by becoming our sin and taking our punishment so we could become right with God.

He who was pure and holy became ugly and dirty, when He took the evil of what we did and are doing, into His body. He who had never known sin, then knew our very sin in His body and soul. This was harder for him to bear than the awful physical torture of crucifixion, for it caused Him to be separated from His Father. Jesus cried out, "My God, my God, why hast thou forsaken me?" (Mark 15:34).

Jesus had never before been separated from His Father. He was and is, "The only begotten Son, who is in the bosom of the Father…" (John 1:18, NKJV). He had always been in His Father. God had to forsake Him when He took our sins into His body. We cannot even imagine the emotional pain and agony and even terror He experienced from being separated from His Father, as well as knowing sin for the first time in His soul.

He became our sins, died with them, and took them to Hell so we would not have to go there. Our Father is holy, Jesus went to the cross that we might be holy like our Father, and that we might live with Him forever in Heaven. Jesus paid the price of death with our sins. "For the wages of sin is death; but the gift of God is eternal life through Jesus Christ our Lord" (Romans 6:23). He was dead, but God raised Him in a new body. That is why we can know we are forgiven because God accepted His Son's sacrifice for us, and when we die, He shall raise us in a new body.

He has taken your punishment, but you must confess, that means taking ownership of and responsibility for your sin against God and hurting the other person or persons whether they were in agreement or not. When you come to God with a humble and repentant heart, He offers forgiveness to you. "If we confess our sins, He is faithful and just to forgive us our sins, and to cleanse us from all unrighteousness" (1 John 1:9).

Speak aloud and tell God you are sorry, naming the sexual sin. In inner healing prayer ask the Lord to meet you in a scene and give you a second chance to say "No" to the sexual sin. With His Almighty Presence there, nothing evil only good can happen. Repent and turn away from ever doing it again, asking Holy Spirit to help you and keep you. Then ask Father to forgive you and cleanse you. Ask Him to tell the other person you are sorry if it's not appropriate for you to tell them and to ask for their forgiveness. If you have or had a spouse and it's appropriate, ask that one to forgive you for breaking your marriage covenant. Finally say out loud, "God forgives me, and I forgive myself, (or say your name)." Write about what Jesus or Father communicated to you, how you felt as God loved you and forgave you. What does it mean for your heart and life to be cleansed of all unrighteousness?

## *My Journal*

### DATE:

*My healing and my forgiveness.*

_____

_____

_____

_____

_____

Chapter 5

If you have a sexual addiction, you may need extended times of inner healing and deliverance with a Christian counselor and/or times spent in conferences, retreats, or groups dealing with such addictions.

Father and Jesus love you so much, and they hate the evil of sexual addiction that ruins their children's lives, both the lives of the abusers and the abused. You were born to be a child of God, conceived anew by His Spirit. You did not start out wanting to be addicted, no one wants to be addicted because addiction makes you its slave. God can and will set you free of sexual addiction, and He has plans to restore and redeem your life.

In inner healing it is necessary to ask God at what age and where the seed of this addiction got planted in you. In counseling, I found that the addiction of pornography sometimes got planted in childhood or pre-teen years by a family member or by older boys. With sexual abuse, the seed often got planted with the person themself being the victim of sexual abuse as a child or young person. As you ask Jesus to be with you in the scene, ask Him to give you the grace to forgive those who planted the seed in you.

All evil has to stop where Jesus is. What is He saying, what is He doing, or what are you feeling with Him there? You may see cool streams of water washing over you. He will wash you with His Word. He gives me His Word for you from Ezekiel 36:25-29 (NKJV), "Then I will sprinkle clean water on you, and you shall be clean; … I will give you a new heart and put a new spirit within you: … I will put My Spirit within you… I will be your God… I will deliver you from all your uncleannesses." You may see Him on the cross taking your sexual sins into His Body and making you clean, giving you back your innocence. You may see the fire of the Holy Spirit burning the sin away or as you see Jesus, you may see light emanating from Him completely dissolving your sexual sin.

## *My Journal*

DATE:

*Where the seed got planted that started my addiction. Those I need to forgive. What Father or Jesus did and what happened to me during my inner healing scene or scenes. If need be, ask God to direct you to the right additional help with counseling, accountability, and groups dealing with addiction.*

_____

_____

_____

_____

_____

_____

_____

_____

_____

_____

_____

The apostle Paul was describing in his letter to the church in Corinth that just as the proper use of food is for nourishment to our bodies through our stomach and that our stomach was made for food, so all of our body including the sexual part is made for the Lord, and the Lord is the spiritual nourishment for our body. Our bodies were not made for the wrong use of sex but to glorify God through the sacrament of marriage.

In Ephesians 5:22-33, we see that the husband is representative of God and the wife is representative of all of us. God wrote Himself into creation when He created marriage. For the husband is to love his wife and be the protector, the nourisher (the provider), and the cherisher of his wife's body as God protects, nourishes (provides nourishment for body, soul, and spirit), and cherishes us. The wife loves her husband through reverencing, honoring, and believing in him as we are to love God. We are given the opportunity in marriage to be the outward and visual sign of our love for God in the way we love our spouse. As we minister the sacrament of the physical union to our spouse, we are fulfilling God's plan in creation to show His ultimate love for us in body, soul, and spirit.

Fornication is participating in sex before marriage. Adultery is participating in sex with another person other than your marriage partner. In either one we are using our body for ourselves or letting others use it for their selves. It breaks God's plan for marriage, the covenant of His love for us and our love for Him. God intended marriage to be for our joy and to be the sweetest and most precious reflection of His love for us as individuals.

When we say our marriage vows, we are saying them to God as well as to the one we are marrying. I will love this person for better or worse, for richer or poorer, in sickness and in health; because you, God love me this way. I am vowing to minister your love and grace to this one I am marrying because you minister love and grace to me. Marriage is a sacrament, an outward and visible sign of an inward and spiritual grace. In marriage each person ministers the sacrament of God's love to the other in the sexual union in a lifetime commitment as God has pledged His eternal commitment to us.

In Ephesians 5:31-32 (NLT), we learn that the two becoming one flesh in marriage is God's great mystery, illustrating the way Christ and the church (Christians) are one. It beckons to what awaits us in the marriage supper of the Lamb and our final consummation with our Lord in Heaven. It is a deeply moving and beautiful illustration, one that we cannot fathom with our mind, but one that speaks to the heart. God wrote Himself into creation when He created marriage.

If you are a person who knew what God says about fornication and adultery or if you did not know, and you used your body or let your body be used in this way, God doesn't condemn you. Jesus came into the world to save our bodies, souls, and spirits. "For God sent not His Son into the world to condemn the world; but that the world through Him might be saved" (John 3:17).

God created the physical union to be like spiritual glue which is a wondrous thing in marriage. It creates a oneness with your marriage partner in the spirit realm which is of the body and beyond body. A husband and wife can actually feel a part of each other even when they are physically separated. God intended this as it speaks of the reflection of His union with us as individuals. No one can take your place in God's heart; you have an intimacy with Him that cannot be broken. "For I am persuaded that neither death nor life, nor angels nor principalities nor powers, nor things present nor things to come, nor height nor depth, nor any other creature, shall be able to separate us from the love of God which is in Christ Jesus our Lord" (Romans 8:38-39).

Heartache and despair come as a result of casual sex or having sex before marriage, you are glued in the spirit to more than one and cannot have that wondrous intimacy which your heart so desires, and which God created for you to have in marriage. Thank God, He can unglue us and set us free!

Sadly, many churches and Christian parents (and I include myself in this group) have not known how or have failed to teach children God's beautiful intention for and meaning of marriage and its sexual component, and by default the culture has left them with Satan's intentions. Youth are now encouraged on every side by magazines, movies, music, TV, social media, and even some schools to experiment with sex, albeit "safe" sex.

The culture's advice to dating couples is to have sex to see if you are sexually compatible before marriage. A prevalent thing in our world today is for couples to simply move in together, saving the money and stress of a marriage celebration and offering a quick exit if things don't work out.

Having sex before marriage causes an unknowable block in one's relationship with God. If you have never had a relationship with Him, it unknowingly causes you to feel that He is not necessary to your life or that He doesn't exist. If you have had a relationship with Him, it can cause you to give up on knowing Him because you think you've already "blown it."

If your heart is hurting because of these things, and you wished you hadn't participated in sex before marriage or after marriage with someone else, then tell God you are sorry. Tell

Him you are sorry for breaking His commandment and hurting Him and hurting the other person or persons who were involved as well as your own body. "Flee fornication. Every sin that a man does is without the body; but he that commits fornication sins against his own body" (1 Corinthians 6:18).

Tell God if you could have a second chance, you would not do it. He will forgive you, and He will give you that second chance in inner healing prayer. Perhaps He will take you back to the scenes; give you the second chance in His Presence and love to say, "No." Every inner healing is different because your life is different from everyone else's life, but God knows you and interacts with you personally. You may need to pray more than once about your relationships with certain people.

If your heart still loves someone that you had a sexual union with, and you are married to another or that person is married to another, your soul and body needs to be set free from that one. Ask God to cause your heart and thus your body to forget how it loved that person. He is the only One who can cause the heart to forget. In inner healing prayer ask Him to come. Make a basket with your palms, put within it anything that was good concerning the relationship, then lift it up to God letting it go to Him, then ask Him to cause your heart to forget how it loved that person and to separate you finally. I don't know how He will do it, but He will do it because it is His will that you be free. You may see Him take His sword of the Spirit and sever the bonds that are holding you.

If you have used your body or others have used it in any way that's not according to God's will, in inner healing prayer pour out your heart to Him, tell Him about it. If you have abused and defiled yourself, He is longing to forgive you. Remember,

"If we confess our sins, He is faithful and just to forgive us our sins, and to cleanse us from all unrighteousness" (1 John 1:9).

God loves you like no other person loves you. You are His child, He is your Daddy, your Abba. Because our bodies belong to Him, sexual defilement defiles Him as well as ourselves.

If with sexual sin you have abused others or yourself or if you have been abused, yes, God is furious about that; because you are His precious child. But Jesus took that abuse and defilement in His own body, and you need to see Him deal with it. In inner healing prayer you may see Him wash it away by His blood, or blow it away, or burn it up by the wind and fire of Holy Spirit, so you can forgive or be forgiven and be free of its effects, so your heart can be healed. "If you forgive anyone's sins, their sins are forgiven; if you do not forgive them, they are not forgiven" (John 20:23, NLT).

Simply ask Him in inner healing prayer to meet you in these situations. Then with the intuitive sense of your spirit see with your mind's eye what God is telling you or doing in the scene to bring forth His will and the healing of your heart. Take Him at His Word for forgiveness. If need be, revisit this scene again with Father or the Lord Jesus until it is established and secured in your memory. The love, light, and holiness of His Presence will become more real to you than the hurtful or evil scene because in the spirit realm His Holy Spirit has wiped it out and brought about His beautiful, loving will for all eternity in your life.

God is always there and ready to give you a new beginning, He makes all things new. "Therefore, if any man be in Christ, he is a new creature: old things are passed away; behold, all are become new" (2 Corinthians 5:17). You will feel new, as if your body had never participated in fornication or adultery or any other sexual sin. Jesus gives us His innocence as our own. He has claimed us as His own and we have accepted His claim so, it's as if we never participated in wrongful sex or were never abused by another or by ourselves.

Write what God did or what He told you, how you felt when you forgave others or when He forgave you. Write how He set you free from multiple sexual partners if that was needed. What did He say and how did you feel about your body when He made it new? Write about your new beginning, your future because now you know God is your good Father. He is your Abba (Daddy), and He will keep you. "Now unto Him that is able to keep you from falling, and to present you faultless before the presence of His glory with exceeding joy" (Jude 24).

## *My Journal*

DATE:

*My New Life.*

_____
_____
_____
_____
_____
_____
_____
_____

Chapter 5

Leviticus 19:28 says, "You shall not make any cuttings in your flesh for the dead nor print any marks upon you…" You probably didn't know this was in the Bible because tattoos are so prevalent in our culture today. But this makes perfect sense, if our body is the Lord's and not our own, we shouldn't mark up someone else's property. We wouldn't go mark up our neighbor's house.

If you have had your body marked with tattoos and your heart is sad about it, just tell God you are sorry. Ask Him to forgive you and tell Him you want your body to be a special place for Him to dwell, a holy place, a place of worship just as a church is a holy place where His Presence is felt. Tell Him you would never mark a church with graffiti, so now in inner healing prayer He can show you your body as His temple where the Holy Spirit dwells. Listen to hear or feel His favor and love upon you. Remember you are special to God. No one can take your place in His heart.

After your inner healing prayer time, as you see the marks, they will simply be the signs that you are forgiven! They will be a remembrance of your time with Jesus or Father! Now you will know that you're looking at an arm or leg, at a hand or foot that belongs to God, a body that is set apart and dedicated to Him.

# *My Journal*

## DATE:

Write about seeing or feeling God, and what He communicated to you and how you feel different about your body.

Knowing what God says about your body and having experienced His love in inner healing prayer, will affect your spouse, your children, your grandchildren, and your friends. Because those around us sense how we feel about our body. Your respect for your body will help others respect their bodies, and you can let them know that their bodies are precious because Jesus died for them, and they belong to God.

Knowing this, we won't criticize our looks, and we won't compare ourselves with others. Our joy is increased because we now understand that our Lord can live with us in our body through our spirit.

You could say, you find yourself living in a house that Someone else has bought but has given you the joy of living in it. This Someone (God) is deeply longing for each one of us to invite Him to come into that house and live with us in the most intimate union and fellowship possible to man. If we invite Him, He will come into our body and live with us through our spirit. "Behold, I stand at the door, and knock, if any man hear my voice, and open the door, I will come into him, and will sup with him, and he with me" (Revelation 3:20).

## *My Journal*

### DATE:

*If you have never yet invited Him to come in, this would be a good time to do it. Say, "Lord Jesus thank you for dying for my sins. Please forgive me and come into me and be my Savior." He saves us from Hell when we die, and we get to go to Heaven to be with Him and Father.*

*Write how you have asked Jesus to come into your spirit and love you, be your friend as well as your Savior and Lord. Write how you now feel about your body.*

# CHAPTER 6

# Inner Healing Prayer and Your Soul and Spirit

Our soul is our psychological nature made up of our mind, emotions, and will. The soul and the spirit of a person are different though they are very closely connected. Hebrews 4:12 tells us that the soul and spirit are connected like the joints and marrow of bones. The spirit is like the marrow, our deep inner being.

"God is a Spirit: ..." (John 4:24). Since God created us in His own image, we are spirit too. When we die our spirit returns to God who gave it (Ecclesiastes 12:7).

Jesus said it is our spirit that must be born again (or conceived anew) by God's Spirit coming into our spirit (John 3:3-6). When you say, "Jesus forgive me my sins, and be my Lord and Savior," God (His Spirit) comes into you, into your spirit, your deep inner being, and births you to Himself. It is your spirit then that is born of God. You then become God's child not just a created being in His image. You have the DNA of your Heavenly Father. That's why your spirit wishes to cry Abba (Daddy) as Jesus did (Mark 14:36). "And because you are sons, God has sent forth the Spirit of His Son into your hearts, crying, Abba, Father" (Galatians 4:6).

Jesus was the firstborn among many brethren (Romans 8:29). When Jesus left Heaven, came to this planet and took our sins on the cross, He made it possible for us also to become the children of God. A Christian's spirit has been impregnated with God's seed (or Spirit). 1 Peter 1:23 says, "Being born again, not of corruptible seed, but of incorruptible…".

1 Corinthians 6:17 says "…he that is joined to the Lord is one spirit. So, then you are always joined to God in your spirit if you have asked Him to be your Lord and Savior. The real you is your spirit person who is the new creature, who is made up of your spirit and God's Spirit together. In the 1970s we use to sing a song about sugar in your tea. When you put the sugar in and it combines with the tea, "You can't take the sugar out of the tea, and you can't take God out of me." This illustrates so well His Spirit coming into our spirit making us one with Him. You still have a body and a soul nature which knows sin, that is the "old man." ("…the old man, which is corrupt… and you put on the new man, which after God is created in righteousness and true holiness" (Ephesians 4:22-24). The new man is your spirit person.

In Hebrews 4:12, we learn that God's Word discerns between the soul and the spirit. Both, His written word (logos) in the Bible and His rhema word spoken to our hearts, discern between the soul and the spirit. His Word discerns the thoughts and intents of the heart. So, as we study the Bible and listen to what Father is telling us in our heart, we will know if a thought, intention, or emotion has its origin in the soul or the spirit. We will know what is coming from our soul and what is coming from our spirit.

In his letter to the church at Rome Paul says, "…when I would do good, evil is present with me. For I delight in the law of God after the inward man (the spirit); but I see another law in my members, warring against the law of my mind, and bringing me into captivity to the law of sin which is in my members" (Romans 7:21-23). He is saying that even though he wants to do that which is right (in his inward man or spirit) he finds that the law of sin in his members (in his soul and body) is warring against the law of his mind (what he knows from his spirit to be right).

After we are born again of God's Spirit, sin still dwells in our soul and body through old habit patterns. We are used to living out of our souls rather than our spirits directing our souls. For the rest of our lives God has us in the wonderful process of sanctification (making holy) our bodies and souls (minds, emotions, and wills). "And the very God of peace sanctify you wholly …" (1 Thessalonians 5:23). He does this by His Spirit within us. "…throw off your old sinful nature and your former way of life, which is corrupted by lust and deception. Instead, let the Spirit renew your thoughts and attitudes. Put on your new nature, created to be like God - truly righteous and holy" (Ephesians 4:22-24, NLT). Holy Spirit renews our minds (souls) as we read and read aloud and meditate on God's Word, the Bible, and as we worship with and find our place in the Body of Christ, the Church.

Inner healing is often called soul healing, or the restoring of the soul. God wants to restore our souls to His original intention. In the 23rd Psalm we read, "He restoreth my soul: he leadeth me in the paths of righteousness for His name's sake" (Psalms 23:3).

In his letter to the Christians in Thessalonica (1 Thessalonians 5:23), Paul prays that our Father God sanctify or make us holy in every part of our spirit, soul, and body. He also says God is faithful, and He will do it, but we must want to be holy in every part of our being as our Father is holy. One of the ways in which we can cooperate with God in this sanctifying process is by inviting Him to come in inner healing prayer, and be known to us where we have been hurt or where we have hurt Him or others. His Presence and love heal our hearts. His Presence and love restore our souls. Then our bodies, minds, emotions, and wills become free from the hurts and effects of the sins of our past.

If we have become subject to one or more addictions, we must take God at His Word and believe He will do for us what we cannot do for ourselves. Inner healing and deliverance from addictions often go together. But we must ask our Father for direction. Each person is different, and He heals and delivers in many ways. He loves you, and He knows just the direction in which you are to go for your healing and deliverance.

## *My Journal*

### DATE:

*Write any addictions you might have and then ask the Lord to come and talk to you about the addiction and ask him for direction. Then write what He tells you.*

_____

_____

_____

1 John 1:8 says, "If we say that we have no sin, we deceive ourselves, and the truth is not in us." 1 John 3:9 (NKJV) says, "Whoever has been born of God does not sin, for His seed remains in him; and he cannot sin, because he has been born of God." We as Christians know we have been born of God's Spirit (His Seed), but we also know that throughout our life we struggle with sin in our members. How can we reconcile these two scriptures? One interpretation is to say that Christians do not practice sin regularly. However, I think we can reconcile them when we understand that the part of us which has been conceived anew and born again of God, our spirit (that incorruptible seed, 1 Peter 1:23) does not sin, but that which was born of the flesh (a Christian's soul and body) still has the old habit patterns of sin which the Bible tells us is our "old man," our old sin nature. We were born with a predisposition to sin and, we have grown up in a world where we have learned to sin.

Saint Paul tells us in Romans 6:6 (NKJV), "… that our old man was crucified with Him (Jesus) … that we should no longer be slaves of sin." But he also says in the 11th verse that we must reckon ourselves to be dead to sin and alive to God in Christ Jesus our Lord.

How do we reckon ourselves to be dead to sin and alive to God in Christ Jesus? We do this by getting to know, to love, and to honor our spirit person, the person that is alive to God in Christ Jesus. The more we know that person the more we want to be that person. She or he is so beautiful, good, and pure like Jesus. We don't want to be the selfish, unkind, unloving person; a slave of sin.

Your spirit person is the person God planned. He chose you to be in and like His Son Jesus before the foundation of the world, to be holy and without blame before Him in love (Ephesians 1:4). That is the person God knew and loved before you were formed in your mother's womb. That one will become more and more real to you as you continue throughout your lifetime having inner healing prayer (and deliverance if necessary) and studying and following with faith God's Word, the logos, His written Word in the Bible and the rhema, His guidance and instructions to you personally which line up with the Bible. We also come to know and experience our spirit person during our personal worship and prayer time and journaling as well as worship with other Christians and finding our place and work in Jesus's Body on earth, the Church.

If we are Christians, we must remember always that we are joined to our Father in Heaven because His Spirit is joined to our spirit (1 Corinthians 6:17). We do not have to be controlled by our old sin nature. Saint Paul describes it this way, "But you are not controlled by your sinful nature. You are controlled by the Spirit if you have the Spirit of God living in you" (Romans 8: 9, NLT). God's Spirit is a living Person inside of you, inside your spirit. The real you, your spirit person reflects His nature because He has put Himself in you, He has impregnated your spirit with His. Even though you sin, there is a part of you that does not want to sin.

It is so important for you to realize there is a part of you that is pure and holy and without sin. That part is the real you, and that is how God sees you. This is important because our enemy, the devil, accuses us night and day and especially if we have addictions. He will try to bring us into condemnation and make us believe that we are really not Christians when we sin with our minds and emotions, or our wills and bodies. Your spirit person, the real you is the person your heart wants to be. That is how God sees you, beautiful, pure, and holy just as He intended you. He sees you washed by the blood of His Son. You are the righteousness of God in Christ Jesus by faith in Him (Romans 3:22).

Always remember that the blood of Jesus once shed on the cross that day outside of Jerusalem was shed for the forgiveness of your past sins, your present sins, and your future sins. When you sin, you must repent, that means you want to turn around and go in the opposite direction. You agree with God that you went the wrong way, and you are truly sorry for it. It means that if you had the chance to live that time over again, you would not do it. It means you love your Father God more than whatever caused you to sin. If this is not the case, but you want it to be, you can pray and ask Holy Spirit to show you Father's great love for you.

In your body, mind, and even in your emotions (your soul nature) you may still want to do it again, but the real you (your spirit) wants to go God's way. Then ask Him for forgiveness by confessing (taking ownership of going against Father's will) and believing that He is faithful to forgive you (Jesus paid the price for your forgiveness). "If we confess our sins, He is faithful and just to forgive us our sins and to cleanse us from all unrighteousness" (1 John 1:9).

Sometimes, we are not sure if what we've done or said was wrong in God's eyes. We can always pray for Holy Spirit to convict us if we have sinned, because that is one of His jobs. And I have often said it is one of the best prayers we can pray. "Lord, Holy Spirit convict us each day of any way that we are not pleasing our Father in Heaven." Father is plenteous in mercy; He will wash our sin away in the blood of Jesus and forget that it ever happened. "As far as the east is from the west, so far has He removed our transgressions from us" (Psalms 103:12, NKJV). "I even I, am He that blots out your transgressions for my own sake; And I will not remember your sins" (Isaiah 43:25, NKJV).

You proclaim the truth about who you are in Christ Jesus. He has paid for and forgiven all of your sins and as long as your heart longs for Him and to be free of sin, you can count on Him to do for you what you cannot do for yourself. Count on Father to conform you, to make you like Jesus. "For whom He foreknew, He also predestined to be conformed to the image of His Son…" (Romans 8:29, NKJV). "For from the very beginning God decided that those who came to Him—and all along He knew who would—should become like His Son…" (Romans 8:29, TLB). He will do this by the Holy Spirit who lives within you.

When a woman becomes pregnant it is not known by others for a time. Even she herself may not know it for a while. The same may be true when God impregnates our spirit and we become a Christian. Those around us may not know it, and even we ourselves may doubt that "it took." When we feel like our old self and when we see the sin within that so easily besets us, our enemy, the devil makes us think we are not a Christian. That new little creature inside, our spirit born of God, needs to be fed on His Word, day and night and strengthened and encouraged by worship with other Christians.

Just as the baby is nourished in the womb and grows bigger, those around the woman begin to know there is a new creature inside. As the young Christian becomes strong in knowing and believing God's Word for himself, as he has prayer fellowship with His Father in Heaven, and as he is in fellowship with other believers, those around will see the new creature.

"Therefore if any man be in Christ, he is a new creature ..." (2 Corinthians 5:17).

In inner healing prayer ask Father, or Lord Jesus, to introduce you to your spirit person. The person He knew before you were born. Jeremiah 1:5 says, "Before I formed you in the womb, I knew you..." Your spirit person was in the womb of God's heart before you were in the womb of your mother. He loved you and He wanted you. You came from Him and you belong to Him.

God had plans for you and me, wonderful, good plans, but He also knew how His plans could go astray because of the brokenness and sin in this world. He provided a way for us to be redeemed and restored from sin and brokenness and all the hurts of our hearts. Jesus was and is the Way. He came to this planet and died for our sin that we might no longer be separated from God, that we might know Him as our Father and know how much He loves us.

Write what your spirit person is like as you get acquainted with her or him and bond emotionally. That one is in God just as Saint Paul in Colossians 3:3 says that we are hid with Christ in God. So, you can love that little being which was you in Father's heart, as well as the mature spirit person God planned for you to be. You can give him or her your loyalty and love.

It is necessary to discern in the morning that the real you is made up of you and God together, your spirit person, then you can live the rest of the day from that center. That is the person God knows and loves and is interacting with, and it's the person you love. Yes, you can love you, that's alright. Jesus said the first commandment is you shall love the Lord your God with all your heart, soul, and mind; and the second is you shall love your neighbor as yourself (Matthew 22: 37-39). The second person you are told to love is yourself. If you don't love yourself, you can't love your neighbor.

You can let yourself be happy. As you love your spirit person, you can be at peace with yourself because God is in you and with you. "…your real life is hidden with Christ in God" (Colossians 3:3, NLT). Let that person, the real you, take over your mind, emotions, will, and body. That is how we walk by the Spirit and are led by the Spirit (Galatians 5:16,18).

Ask Father to show you yourself in the womb of His heart, in His thoughts, in His love. How did God see me, how did God plan me? Can God still see me like the person He planned? Yes! Write about that person, your spirit person, the real you, what she or he is like, and bond emotionally with that one. You can love her or him with the love of God because He is in that one.

Is there a picture in your memory of you as a baby or a toddler or a small child? Sometimes it helps to see a picture of yourself as a small child before you were introduced to or experienced the brokenness which sin has caused in the world. You can better sense the person God knew before you were formed in the womb.

If you are one who was born with a disability, or if something happened during your life to cause you to be disfigured, just know that you were and are perfect in God's heart. If you do not receive your perfect body and mind while here, He has it waiting for you in Heaven. We are all imperfect in some way during this earthly life, but He sees and knows us perfect, the way He intended. He is with us every moment during this journey on earth. The Bible tells us that Jesus came that we might have life and have it more abundantly (John 10:10). Though we are imperfect here on earth, we can still know our

Father God and His love, and that is life abundant. As you ask Father or Jesus to show you your spirit person, you will see yourself complete and perfect.

## *My Journal*

### DATE:

*My spirit person as I was in Father's heart before I was born.*

_____
_____
_____
_____
_____
_____
_____
_____
_____
_____
_____
_____
_____
_____
_____

# CHAPTER 7

# Inner Healing Prayer and the Baptism of the Holy Spirit

What if someone told you that God, Himself could speak to you, and you could speak to Him all day in a language that you could interpret? You would probably think that was too good to be true. Well, it is true, and that is why Jesus commanded His disciples to wait in Jerusalem for their promise from His Father. "…He commanded them not to depart from Jerusalem, but to wait for the Promise of the Father…" (Acts 1:4, NKJV). The promise was the baptism of the Holy Spirit, which would usher them in to a more intimate experience with Him, and it would give them a personal language whereby they could speak to God and He could speak to them at any time of the day or night for the rest of their lives. You too can have this baptism!

John the Baptist said, "I indeed have baptized you with water: but he shall baptize you with the Holy Spirit" (Mark 1:8, NKJV). John was pointing the way toward Jesus who after His crucifixion, resurrection, and ascension would baptize persons in the Holy Spirit. This baptism in the Holy Spirit is a second experience one is to have after being born of God's Spirit.

We learned in the last chapter how Jesus told Nicodemus that we must be born again of God's Spirit in order to enter into the kingdom of God. We learned that God's Spirit comes into our spirit and births us to Himself and to eternal life when we ask Jesus to come into us and be our Savior and Lord.

This couldn't happen to the disciples, or to any of us, until Jesus had taken their sins, and our sins, to the cross and died with them. Through his death and resurrection, He paid the price for all of us to be born again of God's Spirit. Jesus told the disciples on the night before He died that they already knew the Spirit because He was dwelling with them, but He said the Spirit will be in you (John 7:39 and 14:17). After the resurrection when Jesus appeared to the disciples, He breathed on them and said receive the Holy Spirit so then the Spirit was in them. This was their birthday into the Kingdom. But right before He left, and ascended into Heaven, He told them to wait in Jerusalem until they were baptized with the Holy Spirit.

On the Day of Pentecost (the Day of First-fruits) the disciples were in one accord in one place, and "… they were all filled with the Holy Spirit, and began to speak with other tongues, as the Spirit gave them utterance" (Acts 2:4, NKJV). At that time the Jewish festival of Pentecost was taking place in Jerusalem so there were Jews visiting from many nations. They "…were confounded because every man heard them (the Galileans) speak in his own language" (Acts 2:6).

Both historically as on the Day of Pentecost and sometimes in the present day, Christians have spoken and do speak through "tongues" a language that is known by hearers but is not known by the speaker. God in His sovereignty does this that He might speak to a listener.

Once this happened to me when I was telling a neighbor about the Baptism of the Holy Spirit. I spoke in tongues, and she knew what I was saying! I was speaking an old Spanish language that she as a Sephardic Jew understood!

The baptism of the Spirit was and is necessary for all Christians to have, because it is among other things, an enduement of power to witness. The disciples, who were previously afraid with locked doors after the crucifixion, became fearless to the point of death in witnessing for their Lord after they received this baptism. "But you shall receive power after that the Holy Spirit is come upon you: and you shall be witnesses unto me both in Jerusalem, and in all Judea and in Samaria, and unto the uttermost part of the earth" (Acts 1:8).

We are spiritual beings because we have a spirit, but in our natural state we are not so much aware of the two spirit worlds, one of the Holy Spirit and the one of Satan's dark spirit world. The baptism of the Holy Spirit ushers us into a greater awareness of God's Spirit world and gives us discernment about Satan's evil spirit world. This is so important because Satan mixes his evil with good in order to trap people. An example of this is yoga. Many people go to yoga for the good exercise, but they become trapped by the chants and bowing to demons. I previously wrote about the lady who thought she could choose the good from the evil, like from a smorgasbord.

The baptism of the Spirit can be likened to the uncapping of a well of water. The well, being the Spirit, which is already within the Christian. When the uncapping happens the Spirit overflows, and we respond to His love with our voice. It is like telling the person you love the most how much you love them, but not with your intellect. You make syllables with your voice either speaking or singing, and the Spirit guides them into a language which our minds do not understand but our spirit knows. This is called speaking or singing in tongues.

When we ask Jesus to baptize us in the Holy Spirit, sometimes we do not feel anything. But by faith we open our mouths and begin to speak or sing syllables. Holy Spirit then takes over, and we find ourselves speaking or singing a language. We are not speaking or singing with our intellect, but our spirit is speaking or singing mysteries to God. "For he who speaks in a tongue does not speak to men but to God, for no one understands him; however, in the spirit he speaks mysteries" (1 Corinthians 14:2, NKJV).

It becomes an intimate conversation between our heart and God's heart. It is our personal prayer and love language, and it is a great blessing in our personal worship and in our intercessory prayer to God. Many times in our lives, we do not know how to pray for ourselves, our spouses, our children, our nation, or our world; but the Spirit knows and will pray through our spirit if we will pray or sing in tongues. If we are someplace where we cannot pray out loud, we can still allow the Spirit to pray through our spirit with our lips closed.

To some persons, God gives the gift of tongues and the gift of interpretation of tongues, in order that a message from Him might be spoken and interpreted in a church or wherever Christians are assembled. "When you come together, each of you has a psalm, has a teaching, has a tongue, has a revelation, has an interpretation" (1 Corinthians 14:26, NKJV). This is the "gift tongue" and the "gift of interpretation" which is for a different use than what God intends for us in our private devotions and worship.

In the early church of Corinth, the private devotional tongue was being spoken in church without interpretation. This was a misuse of God's gift. People were speaking their own prayer languages, and no one could understand what was being prayed, and it was causing disorder. Saint Paul, in his letter to the Corinthian Christians, had to correct this, saying "Let all things be done decently and in order." He said, "If anyone speaks in a tongue, let there be two or at the most three, each in turn, and let one interpret. But if there is no interpreter, let him keep silent in church, and let him speak to himself and God" (1 Corinthians 14:40 and 27-28, NKJV).

Father wants us all to have our own love language with Him, both to speak mysteries to Him and by which He speaks mysteries to us. Not even our enemy, Satan, can understand tongues for it doesn't come through the intellect but straight from Holy Spirit into our spirit. Father wants us to be able to interpret our tongue or to draw from it like drawing water out of a well, His thoughts, His pictures, His ideas. As Saint Paul says in 1 Corinthians 14:15 (NKJV), "I will pray with the spirit, and I will also pray with the understanding: I will sing with the spirit, and I will also sing with the understanding." This means that God wants us to know what the Spirit is praying.

Father wants us to be able to interpret our tongue for He wants us to be built up and strengthened by what Holy Spirit is praying through us and what our spirit is praying to God. "He that speaks in an unknown tongue edifies (or builds up) himself…" (1 Corinthians 14:4). He will give us the understanding if we will simply ask and quiet our minds and listen in our spirit. It can be a literal translation, but often it is simply the meaning of what we are speaking or singing. We do not try to reason or think it up as it does not come from our intellect.

With my own tongue, a word or two or an idea will come as I seek to interpret, and then if I build on that the full understanding will come.

To counter the risk of coming up with the wrong interpretation, you should always judge it by God's written word, the Bible, and His nature. Just as we should always judge what we experience in inner healing prayer. (This is of more importance if one has been involved previously in the occult). If the interpretation does not agree with the Bible or does not agree with the nature of God as disclosed by His Son, our Lord Jesus, then we know the interpretation is not right. Do not be discouraged though, practice interpreting your tongue, and you will soon know what is from Holy Spirit.

Often, you will be surprised by His communicating His love for you through tongues, so much so that you can hardly believe it. You will be built up and strengthened in faith and better able to pray inner healing prayer. For then you are praying the thoughts and words of God.

In the booklet, *Releasing God's Ideas by Praying in the Spirit*[2], Roxanne Brant states,

> *It is important to realize that God's rivers of revelation can be released into our lives two ways: (1) through interpreting what we speak in tongues, and (2) through receiving into our minds (after we have prayed in tongues) God's ideas in thoughts, mental pictures, impressions or knowings.*

Jesus said in John 7:38 (NKJV), "He who believes in me, as the scripture has said, out of his heart will flow rivers of living water."

When a person is baptized in the Holy Spirit, there is not only the gift of power to witness, but a magnifying of God's goodness and His greatness in our hearts. "…we do hear them speak in our tongues the wonderful works of God." And "…the gift of the Holy Spirit had been poured out on the Gentiles also. For they heard them speak with tongues and magnify God" (Acts 2:11 and 10:45-46).

This experience greatly increases our desire for the Word of God, the Bible; and it is the beginning of a lifetime of love with our Lord. It is tremendously important in inner healing prayer because it helps us to know and trust God's love. It becomes easier to invite Him into our dark moments, our most ashamed of secrets, and our terrifying scenes for we know God's power is greater than anything or anyone, and that He loves us. He wants to heal us where Satan has tried to hurt us.

In my own life, I grew up in church, so I knew intellectually that God loved me, and I believed that He spoke to the people in the Bible. However, I did not understand that He still speaks to people today, and that one could have an intimate and personal love with Him this side of Heaven. When I experienced the baptism of Holy Spirit, waves of His love filled my body, and I heard Him speak to me. He said He would love persons through me, and that I would never have to feel alone again or afraid again for, "Lo I will be with you always."

At that time, I was not married and working as a social worker for my church. My work included visitation in the city and county jails, as well as visitation with families in poverty situations. It was a great comfort when the Lord told me He would love people through me, as well as His promise to be with me always.

If you have never experienced the second blessing of Holy Spirit, and yet you have asked Jesus to be your Lord and Savior, now He wants to baptize you in His Spirit!

Perhaps you have attended a church which taught that speaking in tongues was not for this age, or it's only for a special few people, or it is from the devil and something to fear. This could be a barrier that will keep you from receiving this wonderful blessing. You will need to renounce the teaching, but you are not renouncing people or churches. As always, we are called to walk in love and seek unity with fellow Christians.

Before you pray for the baptism of the Holy Spirit, if there has been influence in your life from the evil spirit world, you simply need to renounce out loud, one by one those things pertaining to Satan's spirit world.

They would include seeking to gain supernatural knowledge by any means other than by our Lord, or to be guided by it. These would include occult or psychic practices such as ESP, clairvoyance, telepathy, Ouija boards, spiritism, horoscopes, or any type of witchcraft. It would also include any involvement with groups which deny that Jesus is God come in the flesh and that His shed blood on the cross is all that is needed for the forgiveness of our sins. These groups would include the cult religions as well as the pagan religions. In Deuteronomy 18:10 (NLT), God tells us these things are detestable to Him, "…who practices divination or sorcery, interprets omens, engages in witchcraft, or casts spells, (hypnotism) or who is a medium or spiritist who consults the dead."

In our modern- day, hypnotism is intended to help the person being hypnotized, the mind is put in a passive, receptive state which leaves it open to Satan's evil spirits. Such influence can last for years, and the person may need deliverance to be free. Such a person came to me seeking inner healing for the problems in her life, but what she really needed was deliverance from a spirit which entered when she had been hypnotized.

Also, other techniques that are intended for healing can leave one open to the evil spirit realm. These would include New Age practices in healing like those used in seeking or guiding spiritual energy coming from the body. We don't delve in the spirit realm unless we are protected and guided by Holy Spirit and our relationship with the Lord Jesus Christ. There are clinics and businesses everywhere that advertise and promote all types of healing of the body and mind by spiritual means, but they have no relationship to the One who died on the cross saving us from all spiritual darkness, demons, and the devil, himself. In the spiritual realm there is no neutral plane, (such as is believed by many) only that of Holy Spirit and that of Satan.

The reason that one needs to renounce these practices or involvement, even if they were in the past, is to rid yourself of any of their influence. You must call them for what they are, a sin against your Father God, because you were seeking supernatural help by means other than through Him. Even though in innocence, you may have sought them for good and for healing, they leave you open to Satan's spirit world. When you renounce them one by one and ask Father to forgive you, Jesus's blood will cleanse you and rid you of all their influence. And as you have asked Jesus to be your Savior, you are now ready to ask Him to baptize you in the Holy Spirit.

As was stated in the beginning of this chapter, Jesus said in the book of Acts 1:4 that the baptism of the Holy Spirit is a promise from Father. As you quiet your mind and heart, remember you are asking Jesus to give you your promise from Father God.

Say, "Come Lord Jesus and baptize me in the Holy Spirit." Talk to Him, tell Him whatever is in your heart, maybe how much you love Him or want to love Him, maybe how thankful you are that He died for you on the cross and has forgiven all your sins. Be still and know that He is God, draw near to Him and He will draw near to you and you will feel His Presence in you or all around you. Begin to speak or sing your love to Him in syllables, not in your own language, and Holy Spirit will form it into a language, which is called in the Bible "a tongue." "And they were all filled with the Holy Spirit and began to speak with other tongues as the Spirit gave them utterance" (Acts 2:4, NKJV).

You will not understand it with your intellect, but your spirit will know. Some people feel great emotion when they experience the baptism of the Spirit, others do not, but you will know that the baptism is real when you speak in tongues even if it's only a syllable or two. Some persons I have known were diligent to practice speaking the few syllables they were given at first, later they received their full Spirit language.

Write about it, what you felt, what happened, how you experienced the Lord. Were you able to give voice to syllables like when a baby begins to speak, and then did Holy Spirit form it into a language? Remember it's all your own, a special language that Father is giving you to communicate with Him. It's for your edification which means, He's giving it to you for your joy and happiness to build you up (to edify you) and let you know that He loves you and is always with you. "… he who speaks in a tongue does not speak to men but to God…

He who speaks in a tongue edifies himself…" (1 Corinthians 14: 2,4, NKJV).

Practice talking to Father and Jesus every day in your Holy Spirit language especially when you are feeling down and discouraged. Speak in tongues what your heart wants to say to God, then listen for the interpretation. Speak in tongues what you want to hear from God. As you listen in your spirit for words, thoughts, or pictures the interpretation will come. Even though at first you only have fragments, speak aloud these words in your own language, you will be comforted and encouraged. As you practice, interpretation will become easier. Holy Spirit can cheer you up with just one word, one sentence, a thought, or a picture interpreted. He can give you direction for the day, He can warn you when you might be in danger, He can help you when you don't know what to do.

Of course, there will be times when you will want to sing or speak in tongues in pure adoration not wanting to break the worship with interpretation. In the coming days, come back to this page and write about how this experience with Holy Spirit is changing your life, what are the differences it is making?

## *My Journal*

### DATE:

*My experience of receiving the Baptism of the Holy Spirit.*

_____

_____

_____

# CHAPTER 8

# Inner Healing Prayer and Your Prenatal Months and Birth

When you were in the womb, you were a tiny human being that God already knew. Your spirit was present though your body was just being formed. God tells us that He knew us before we were formed in the womb. This is what He told Jeremiah. "Before I formed you in the womb, I knew you: Before you were born, I sanctified you: I ordained you a prophet to the nations" (Jeremiah 1:5, NKJV). Whether your mother's egg and father's sperm came together in the womb or in a test tube, God knew you before!

Even before He made the world, God loved you and chose you to be His through what Jesus would do for you on the cross. "Even before he made the world, God loved us and chose us in Christ to be holy and without fault in His eyes" (Ephesians 1:4, NLT).

It is greatly comforting to know that we were in our Father God's thoughts, we were in the womb of His heart of love before we were ever in our mother's womb. He wanted you; He planned you, He ordained a place for you and your purpose on earth before you were born. And that plan included a victorious life through His Son, Jesus. "I have come that they (you) might have life, and that they (you) might have it more abundantly" (John 10:10, NKJV).

Here are some situations which could cause you to need inner healing prayer for the prenatal months and birth. There were health problems before, during, or after your birth. You knew that you were not planned or wanted by your biological parents. You were conceived by rape, or when your parents were not married, or when it was a very difficult time in their lives. When you were in the womb, one or both of your parents were practicing alcoholics, or were dependent on drugs, or were practicing witchcraft or other occult things. There was a major tragedy that occurred in your mother's life during the pregnancy such as the death of a loved one, domestic violence, the violence of war, or a serious illness.

As I stated at the beginning of this book some situations are so major, to come to healing one must hear from God Himself. He brings peace to the question "why," and He brings reconciliation and wholeness. But that is what inner healing prayer is all about, it's prayer with the expectancy of an experience with one's heavenly Father. It is in His Presence and love that our questions are answered, that our hearts can be truly healed.

If your natural parents chose not to raise you or if other circumstances kept you from being raised by them, the Lord says He will take you up. "Even if my father and mother abandon me, the Lord will hold me close" (Psalms 27:10, NLT). You have a special place in God's heart.

If you don't know who your father was or if he died or deserted the family during your childhood, then something special has happened between you and God. He has declared that He will take the place of your father both on earth and in Heaven. Psalms 68:5 says He will be a father to the fatherless. Jesus said when we pray, we are to call God "Our Father" (Matthew 6:9). The night before His crucifixion in the Garden of Gethsemane He cried out to His Father saying, "Abba (Daddy) Father, all things are possible for You, take this cup away from Me; nevertheless, not what I will, but what you will" (Mark 14:36, NKJV).

Ask Holy Spirit to let you sense yourself in Father's heart as He thought about you, before there was any part of you formed. Let Father love you. He wanted you; He sees you perfect just as He planned. Let Father give you your sense of being as you sense Him calling you into being and as you sense His pride in your being. No one else knows you like He knows you, no one else loves you and cares for you like He loves and cares for you. You came from Him and will return to Him. "… and the spirit shall return unto God who gave it" (Ecclesiastes 12:7).

When you sense yourself in God's heart, embrace that one, hold her or him with your whole being for that is the real you, the one God knows. With joy and celebration and wonder thank Him for your beautiful creation, as did King David in Psalms 139:14, " I will praise thee; for I am fearfully and wonderfully made: marvelous are thy works; and that my soul knoweth right well."

The one you must remember for the rest of your life is the one you really are. When you pray to your Abba Father (Daddy God), put yourself in remembrance of that one (your true self-identity). That is the one praying to your Father, for that is how God sees and knows you. We can get dirty by sin but that doesn't change how God sees us as a son or daughter or as an intended son or daughter. When you accepted Jesus as your

Lord and Savior, God's Spirit literally came into your spirit, and you were born to God. You became His child, not just created by Him in His image but born to Him. But even before you accepted the Lord Jesus, God the Father chose (adopted) you to be His son or daughter.

We can and must ask forgiveness for sin and repent, for that will keep us from knowing His Presence and fulfilling His plan and destiny for us. But our sins do not change God's love for us. As soon as we turn our face and heart toward Him and ask for forgiveness, He takes us in His arms of love.

This is so well illustrated in the story Jesus told of the prodigal son in Luke 11:32. The son had taken his inheritance from the father and wasted it in riotous living and ended up feeding pigs. He went home to his father and said, "…I am no more worthy to be called thy son." But his father saw him coming from afar, ran to him, kissed him, and called the servants to make a celebration, for His son had come home. When you accepted Jesus as your Savior and Lord, your Heavenly Father knows you at all times as His son or daughter, whom He loves, that is your identity.

If there are things you need to be healed of from the prenatal months and birth, let Holy Spirit show you yourself as a tiny babe in your mother's womb. Jesus's gentle but nail scared hands are around your little body. Psalms 139:13 says, "… you have covered me in my mother's womb." He's there protecting you and letting you know how much He loves you. The nail scars in His hands mean that He has gone before you and won every battle that you will face. They are His victory marks for you.

As you are quiet, He may bring to your mind pictures, thoughts, or feelings. The little babe in the womb may feel afraid, unwanted, or rejected. Let Jesus speak His truth into baby's heart. Your little body and life were planned by Father in Heaven, and you are greatly loved and wanted. No one can take your place in His heart, and you were chosen to be His before the foundation of the world (Ephesians 1:4).

He knows you will go through some very difficult times in this world, but He's gone ahead of you, and He will be there for you. You will not have to go through anything alone. On the cross He won for you the victory over all sin and evil. Because He lives, you can live, you can be born. You can choose life. He will never leave you nor forsake you (Hebrews 13:5).

Jesus says you are a member of His body, of His flesh and of His bones (Ephesians 5:30). Now as you accept the gift of life from your Father, God, accept also that little babe which is yourself. Decide to always be his or her friend just as Jesus will always be that one's best friend. And if need be, forgive your mother or father, ask Jesus to show you your parents at your birth, completely healed, saved from their own brokenness, and receiving you with joy as their precious child, a gift from God. "Children are a gift from the Lord; they are a reward from Him" (Psalms 127:3, NLT). Let Jesus call those things which be not as though they were (Romans 4:17).

## *My Journal*

DATE:

*How Father showed me my real self when I was in the womb of His heart. The plans or dreams He had for my future. What was my real self like? Describe her or him.*

*How I emotionally bonded with that one, and will remember for the rest of my life, that is who I am, a son or daughter of the living God, my Father.*

*How God healed my prenatal months and birth.*

*How His love and Presence has brought peace to my question "why."*

# CHAPTER 9

# Inner Healing Prayer and Your Childhood Years

Little children are at a disadvantage when things go wrong in their lives. The young child's mind has not developed enough to understand the reasons behind the circumstances of their lives. An example would be when parents die or are divorced, the child often feels it is his or her fault and will grow up carrying this false guilt. They can also feel it is a personal rejection of themselves. The repressed hurts and fears of childhood are often the things that hobble us emotionally as adults. Is your heart hurting because of something that happened when you were a child?

Rita Bennett in her book, *You Can Be Emotionally Free*,[3] says, "People who greatly dislike themselves in childhood are those with self-identity problems. Others may not actively dislike the child they were, but still have hurts and bad memories that need to be healed."

These hurts and fears of childhood may be so repressed that you have no conscious idea of what they are or when they happened. If so, take the time in a quiet place and ask Holy Spirit by starting when you were very young and going through the different time frames of your childhood to bring up that which you need to address in inner healing prayer. Sometimes God brings them to our attention through dreams, usually not a literal interpretation of the dream but the symbolic interpretation of the heart.

## *My Journal*

DATE:

*Write the things that hurt your heart when you were a child.*

I was one of those persons who, as an adult, looked back and greatly disliked myself as a child. But by God's mercy and grace through inner healing prayer I have learned to love the child that I was, and my true identity was restored. Surely God redeemed my life.

My story is not so different or unique, it is a familiar story that has happened to many. Being the last child of four, my father was hoping for another son, as my older brother had not fulfilled my father's dreams. He was hoping for a son who would love the things he loved, baseball, hunting, and fishing. I received his name, Shade, and I knew very early in childhood that I was to be a son.

By the time I was six I had rejected the clothes and toys of girls for those of a boy. As my childhood progressed, I played football with neighborhood boys, and learned how to fish and hunt with my father. He was my hero, every day I could hardly wait until he came home from work. I would get my mitt and hard ball so we could play catch, and he could teach me to throw a curve. At that time changing gender was unheard of, and for that I am grateful.

When I was eleven almost twelve, my aunt and uncle took me to a special service at our church. The Holy Spirit touched my heart. I wanted to give my life to Jesus. This I did, and He came into me and changed me. He put new loves, new thoughts, new delights in my heart. I began reading the Bible and books about the Lord. Church and my youth group became important to me. My thirteenth year was one of the best of my life, and in the high school years my identity was right and secure.

I never wanted to revisit my childhood; the memories were haunting. I did not like the person I was. I wished to disown her completely, but God in His mercy had something else in mind.

After my husband and I had learned about inner healing prayer, one day he said, "Shade, I think the Lord wants to show you something." Having no idea what he meant, I knelt by the bed and waited on my Father God.

A picture came to mind from long ago, it was me about nine years old playing football with the neighbor boys in a muddy yard. Then the scene changed, the adult me was there alone with Jesus. He told me I had thrown away something in the mud that day. He had carefully picked it up, cleaned it and put it away for safekeeping.

Jesus tenderly gave me back what I had thrown away. I opened the box and found a beautiful white satin wedding gown! He said I had tried to throw away my womanhood, but He had saved it. Shocked! I asked Him to forgive me. He caught me up in His love. Never before had I felt of inestimable worth. I felt myself precious like that beautiful wedding gown, I felt loved, I felt forgiven. In that moment I saw myself through His eyes, I was cherished, I was beautiful. I thanked Him mightily for saving my womanhood.

In a later inner healing prayer, I revisited the scene with the nine-year-old. Jesus was there, and He was walking home with her. He put His arm around her and told her He understood why she felt and acted the way she did. He understood why she wanted to play football with the boys, but He told her who she really was and who she was going to be in the future. Jesus told her He had something wonderful for her in the future, and she would love it!

When she saw the person she was going to be, she wanted to be that one. The adult me was standing in the shadows behind them. Because I saw her responding to Jesus's love and wanting to be that one He was showing her, I could love her. I forgave her. I had never been able to do this before.

Jesus loves us when we cannot love ourselves. He forgives our former selves, when we can't forgive. I can love the child I was because Jesus loved her. He helped me understand the "why" of her behavior. In inner healing prayer He called into being things that were not as if they were, (my real self) and the things which are not to bring to nothing the things that are (my playing football with the boys) (Romans 4:17 and 1 Corinthians 1:28). He made my heart tender as I saw His love for my childhood self. I could forgive her. She was restored in my heart. I no longer was ashamed of that child, and I no longer disowned that part of me. Jesus and Father brought reconciliation.

If you are one of those persons who dislikes the child you were, then in inner healing prayer let God pull back the curtain on eternity and heal your heart.

Ask Father, "What scene do you and Jesus want to meet me in to heal my heart? Help me to understand and love the child I was. Help me to forgive my childhood self. If things happened in my family with my parents or my siblings that hurt me, come Lord Jesus to that scene or scenes and heal my heart. Help me to forgive anyone who caused me to be the way I was as a child."

Remember when you forgive someone, it doesn't mean that what they did was right, or you are excusing it. It means that you are not charging or asking God not to charge it against them. You are accepting that Jesus paid the price for their wrong against you.

If there was a divorce or death or something else of a serious nature, you may need to give the Lord more time in prayer sessions to bring peace and restoration to your heart. Sometimes inner healing happens quickly, at other times it requires more prayer with God. Be willing to commit to the time it takes for God to heal your heart. He is always at work healing our heart even when we don't know it. We wake up some day realizing our heart is healed, a certain matter doesn't hurt anymore!

## *My Journal*

DATE:

*My inner healing prayer asking Jesus or Father to be with me when I was a child and to heal my child's heart.*

_____

_____

_____

_____

_____

_____

_____

_____

_____

_____

# Chapter 9

Mark 10:13-16 tells about Jesus and little children. "Then they brought little children to Him that He might touch them; but the disciples rebuked those who brought them. But when Jesus saw it, He was greatly displeased and said to them, "Let the little children come to me, and do not forbid them; for of such is the kingdom of God. Assuredly, I say to you, whoever does not receive the kingdom of God as a little child will by no means enter it." And He took them up in His arms, laid His hands on them, and blessed them."

Jesus loved the children, and He loves them now. There is a Sunday school song that expresses this so well. "Jesus loves the little children, all the children of the world, … they are precious in His sight …".

Saint Paul tells fathers not to provoke their children to anger, lest they be discouraged (Colossians 3:21). Jesus said, "And whosoever shall offend one of these little ones that believe in me, it is better for him that a millstone were hanged about his neck, and he were cast into the sea" (Mark 9:42). So, we learn that it is a very grave sin to hurt, abuse, or to cause a child to sin especially a child who believes in Jesus.

How does this happen? It can happen by anyone who is given the care of children such as parents, stepparents, grandparents, teachers, and others in supervision of children, or by people who are drawn by demonic spirits to abuse children. It can happen by physical abuse such as discipling in rage, by sexual abuse, by emotional abuse such as teasing, mocking, cursing, belittling, and breaking their spirit, by neglecting or rejecting them, by shaming, or simply being unkind and mean. They can teach children the vices of the world such as pornography, other sexual sins, witchcraft, drunkenness, and killing (as in warfare). The devil hates what God loves, he hates children, and he is about destroying their lives early.

All of these are grievous sins. If you have abused a child in any of these ways, God wants to forgive you. He does not want you to go to Hell carrying that sin (that millstone) around your neck. It is likely that you, yourself, were abused as a child, but God will stop this sin from continuing down the generations. Any and all sins have to stop at the cross because Jesus took them into His own body.

In your heart, go to the cross, see Jesus hanging there in His agony, taking your wretched sin, the sin you've done to others as well as the sins that were done to you, taking that very abuse into His own body. Let it go into Him. Tell Him how sorry you are that you damaged that child or those children. Ask Him to forgive you, and to forgive those who have hurt you. With your will repent (that means turn around and go in the opposite direction), telling God you never want to abuse in any way one of His little ones. Then listen in your heart for His words. Something miraculous can now happen.

Therefore, if you confess your sin against a child or children, (actually you are confessing a sin against God your Father) He is faithful and just to forgive you, and to cleanse you of all unrighteousness (John 1:9). You have been forgiven and your sin is no more.

If there is a demonic spirit continuing to control your mind and body, ask God through inner healing prayer how the spirit came. It could have come when you were a child or youth through abuse done to you. Sin causes sin. Our human response can be anger, fear, rebellion, or judgement. This evil then becomes imprinted on our hearts whereby evil spirits can come. Thank God, Jesus has made a way for us to forgive and be set free.

In inner healing prayer when you experience God's Presence at that time, the time when you were sexually abused or the time whenever the emotional hook took place, He will catch you up in His love and mighty protection. He will burn up, dissolve, or annihilate the evil that is happening to you and the evil in the one or ones who are injuring you. As you see that one who abused you with God burning the evil up or taking it away and out of him or her, you can forgive. When this happens, Jesus or Father can take the evil of the abuse which was imprinted on your heart away. He will burn that evil completely away, cleansing your heart. You will have a new clean heart that will feel like dancing.

Follow the steps for deliverance, naming the spirit or spirits, binding them by the blood and name of Jesus and sending them to Hell never to return to you or this planet. You often feel delivered by the exhaling of breath. Then ask Father what He is giving you in place of that evil thing. Sometimes He will put a picture or word in your mind of the new gift. As Isaiah 61:1-3 tells us that God anointed Jesus "…to proclaim liberty to the captives, and the opening of the prison to them that are bound; …to give unto them beauty for ashes…" If you feel you need extra help with counseling or deliverance prayers, ask God to lead you to the right person or place for this help.

Jesus has set you far apart from that which was done to you, and that which you have done. He has annihilated the sin which was done to you and/or the sin which you did. You will no longer have to experience fear, anger, rebellion, or feel like a victim. You will not be dogged by a spirit of victim mentality, or by an evil sexual picture in your mind, or by evil sexual feelings in your body. You will not have to keep fighting back at the world or repeating the abuse upon others to make things right. God has made things right for you. You are God's beloved son or daughter; He has set you free! "If the Son therefore shall make you free, you shall be free indeed" (John 8:36).

## *My Journal*

DATE:

*In your inner healing time, journal what is appropriate to you if you were the one abused or if you were the abuser. What I saw in my inner healing and deliverance, how God took the evil away from me, how He took it away from the one or ones that abused me. My deliverance, and what God gave me in place of the evil spirit or spirits that I cast into Hell. What God told me and how I felt as His beloved son or daughter.*

Not only do adults sin against children, but children sin against one another. Proverbs 22:15 tells us that foolishness is bound in the heart of a child. Though babies look sweet and innocent, the child soon begins to show evidence that we are all a fallen human race. If young children are not supervised closely, one will hit another or snatch a toy away from a playmate. Selfishness begins to be exhibited as one child tries to hoard toys or food for him or herself. Older children may tease or "make fun" of younger ones or those who have disabilities or deformities or those who look or sound different from themselves. "Bullies" may intimidate or physically abuse smaller children.

Though foolishness is bound in the heart of a child, Proverbs 22:15 also says the rod of correction shall drive it far from him. There are times and places for proper correction in all of our lives and especially when we are children. Ephesians 6:1 and 4 says, "Children, obey your parents in the Lord: for this is right." "And you fathers, provoke not your children to wrath: but bring them up in the nurture and admonition of the Lord."

We are to discipline our children, not in anger and not when we are out of control, but with the purpose of training them rather than punishing them. We are to train them for the Lord's sake, for our children belong to God, not to us. We are His stewards of their lives. "Train up the child in the way he should go: and when he is old, he will not depart from it" (Proverbs 22:6).

If we fail to discipline our children, that also is a type of abuse, for they grow up not knowing right and wrong and believing that they are gods of their own lives. In the Old Testament, Eli a priest did not discipline his sons. God told him, "…I will judge (your) house for ever for the iniquity which (you) know: because (your) sons made themselves vile, and (you) restrained them not" (1 Samuel 3:13).

If you remember as a child hurting other children by hitting, teasing, bullying, or any other way, God wants to wash your heart clean of that. If you are a parent and remember disciplining when you were out of control or disciplining to punish, God wants to wash your heart clean and forgive you. If you are a parent who could not or did not discipline, and your child or children grew up to be rebels thinking they were their own gods having to learn the lessons of life the hard way, God wants to forgive you. He can still heal your heart and heal your children through inner healing prayer.

If you fit any of these situations, give God the opportunity to not only bring healing to your heart, but to your children or others that were affected. Ask Him to come into the scene or scenes that are relevant. Watch and let Him (His Presence and love) make things right. Ask for forgiveness or give forgiveness where needed and journal what He did or said or what happened in the scenes. Remember, others do not have to know they were in the scenes when you prayed inner healing prayer, but what is happening is affecting them in the spirit realm because God's Holy Spirit is at work changing lives for good.

# *My Journal*

## DATE:

*How God brought healing to me as a child or parent. What He said or did, and how others in the scenes were affected.*

There are circumstances which mar a child's heart over which parents have no control. War, with all its horror, often causes children to suffer the most. Some have seen their parents killed, raped, or maimed. Some have been maimed or disfigured themselves by bullets, mines, or missiles. And some have had to flee their homes and live in refugee camps. Lastly, some children have never had enough to eat or proper clothes to wear. All of these things make it so difficult to grow up without emotional scars.

Our hearts cannot bear the assault of violence. To survive the horror, we have to repress these assaults on our souls or disassociate ourselves until such time as we can walk back to them in the Presence and love of our Lord Jesus. But God in His mercy gave and gives to us Jesus: our Brother, our Friend, our Savior. Jesus comes to us all, to the little child as well as to the adult.

He is altogether lovely, altogether pure and holy, and altogether strong. He is the Good Shepherd. If you are one who as a child had your heart marred by any of these situations, perhaps you have repressed specific memories, and yet you have experienced deep depression and suicidal thoughts, let Him hold the little child you were, like a lamb to His bosom. You are covered in His pure white robe, and He is holding your little face in His hand. He is brushing away your tears and taking all the hurt and fear from your heart and putting it into His heart. He covers your eyes, and that bad thing that happened goes into His nail-scarred hand. You will never have to look upon it again. Your ear is pressed against His chest, and you can hear His heartbeat. You know it is beating for you because you belong to Him now. You are not alone, and you will never be alone again. You will never have to be afraid again. Listen for His words in your heart. You are His and He is yours forever, He will never leave you nor forsake you (Hebrews 13:5).

Take time to be in Jesus's arms and rest, until your little child's heart is healed. The memory of the situation that marred your heart may surface. If it does, you do not have to be afraid because Jesus is there taking care of you.

## *My Journal*

DATE:

*How Jesus healed my child's heart. What He said, and how I felt to be in His arms and with Him.*

_____

_____

_____

_____

_____

_____

_____

_____

_____

_____

_____

_____

Jesus has set you free, free to respond to life the way He intends it, not the way you have experienced it. Can you offer that same freedom to the one or ones who abused or hurt you? Can you ask God to forgive their sin against you? If so, pray this prayer.

> *"Dear Father, I take your big eraser and erase the charge against (name the person or persons or country if there was a war) who hurt me so badly. I forgive them and ask you to forgive them and set them free from their sin and hurt against me. And now set me free from any and all harm that I have experienced because of it. I take the blood of Jesus and cover that sin, and His blood separates me forever from it."*

When we do this, we are free, we are no longer bound as a victim by the hurt done to us. It opens up a clear passageway in the spirit realm between God and the person or persons who hurt us, and God can bring redemption to them. It also fulfils what Jesus told us to pray, "For if you forgive men their trespasses, your Heavenly Father will also forgive you…" (Matthew 6:14).

Then great and mighty things can happen as in John 29:23, "If you forgive the sins of any, they are forgiven them; if you retain the sins of any, they are retained." And Matthew 18:18 says, "Assuredly, I say unto you, whatever you bind on earth will be bound in Heaven, and whatever you loose on earth will be loosed in heaven." Jesus has won! The Kingdom of God has come in your life on earth as it is in Heaven. God's will has been done! "Your kingdom come, your will be done on earth, as it is in Heaven" (Matthew 6:10, NKJV).

CHAPTER 10

# Inner Healing Prayer and Your Teen and Early Adult Years

The teenage years have often been described as the most difficult years of our lives. Our struggle to find our identity and secure our independence often produces heartache with parents and siblings, as well as a greater than normal temptation to sin. Our vulnerability to peer pressure is greater than at any other time in life. There is a desperate need to have someone we can trust to understand what we are feeling and to help us sort out those feelings. It is a tender, sensitive age; an age when we want so much to believe in someone. Heroes and heroines are commonplace but so is disillusionment and broken dreams. Is it no wonder the author of Psalms 25:7 said, "Remember not the sins of my youth…".

Many of the hurts of childhood are repressed out of consciousness, but the hurts of the teenage and early adult years are usually those we remember the most. Because of this, we may dislike and be estranged from our teenage self. If that is true, our adult person needs to be reconciled with the self of our youth. With Jesus and through His love and tender understanding, our adult person can love and accept, and if need be, forgive the teenager we were. "Remember, O Lord, thy tender mercies and thy loving kindnesses; for they have been ever of old (Psalms 25:6).

A woman came to me who was distraught over the sins of her youth. She had become pregnant in her teens. She was not married, and abortion was not legal. This young girl despaired of having her baby. She attempted to kill the baby by not eating or drinking and ended up in the hospital.

We invited the Lord Jesus to walk back with her to that day. Together they walked into the hospital room. Jesus looked with compassion and love upon that frightened teenager. Then the adult woman and Jesus together embraced the young mother and offered forgiveness to her. Tears that had been locked up for years flowed. Never again would that desperate young girl be separated or hated in the heart of the adult woman, for Jesus had brought love, forgiveness, and reconciliation.

See what Colossians 1:20-22 (NKJV) tells us about reconciliation. "...by Him to reconcile all things to Himself, by Him, whether things on earth or things in heaven, having made peace through the blood of His cross. And you, who once were alienated and enemies in your mind by wicked works, yet now He has reconciled in the body of His flesh through death to present you holy, and blameless, and above reproach in His sight."

Through inner healing prayer the Lord Jesus, Himself came and brought love and forgiveness to the frightened teenager so the adult woman could forgive her and be reconciled. This woman did not have to spend the rest of her life being distraught over the sins of her youth.

Are there wrong choices you made as a youth or situations which cause you pain as you think about them? Remember

God can and wants to heal your heart concerning things that happened during those years. Write these things in your journal or on the blank page, and then ask Father God or Lord Jesus to come and be with you in those times of your youth.

Jesus loved you, and He understood even when no one else could. Let your teenage self pour out his or her heart to the Lord. He was there, He knows and felt acutely the pain and the injustice that happened to you if you were abused. He believes in you even if you made wrong choices. He is the God of the "second chance," and He will give you that "second chance" in inner healing prayer. Ask Him to come and be with you in those scenes. Let yourself feel His Presence and love, and He will heal your heart so that you will not carry those scars any longer!

## *My Journal*

### DATE:

*How Father or Jesus met me when I was a young person. What He did or said and how my heart was healed.*

_____

_____

_____

_____

_____

_____

# CHAPTER 11

# Inner Healing Prayer for Your Children and Yourself as a Way of Life

Throughout life, circumstances happen that cause us and our children to need inner healing prayer. What comfort to know that our Lord is always available and longing to heal us.

It is easy to pray with children for they have not built up the intellectual prejudice and other resistance of adults. They are eager to believe, and they are open to the Presence of the Lord. They can readily see or feel the Lord Jesus in the scene. You can begin praying inner healing prayer with your children or grandchildren as soon as they know the name of Jesus. And, of course, you can begin praying for them (seeing Jesus with them) as soon as you know they are in the womb.

One winter my son was playing in the snow near our driveway, when an angry man came along looking for someone who had broken his window with a snowball. He mistakenly thought our son was the culprit, and with a stick in his hand the man told my son he was going to kill him. Our child ran to the door as fast as he could, and I found him there screaming and shaking terribly. I had never seen him so frightened. Immediately, we called upon the name of Jesus. I asked Jesus to make Himself known to my child as he was in the snow at the time the man appeared.

My son saw the Lord and he said, "Mama, Jesus is bigger than the man with the stick!" Jesus won; Satan lost! Our child's fear was diffused, and Satan had no chance to cause him harmful repercussions the rest of his life from this incident. Only the Presence of Jesus could have taken away that kind of fear. I couldn't have talked my child out of it. As an adult, he served in the armed forces during war and volunteered to lead many missions in harm's way without fear.

I have thanked God through the years for the gift of praying inner healing prayer with my children.

Many times, in my own life, I have closed my eyes, quieted my heart, and asked Jesus to let me see or feel His Presence in whatever scene or moment there was hurt. His Presence has brought me healing over and over again. Sometimes just seeing Him, His great power, light, and love in a scene of darkness was enough to heal my soul. At other times I needed to hear His words, those words that are quick and powerful and sharper than a two-edged sword, words that pierce right through our confusion and set us free. See Hebrews 4:12.

I John 4:8 tells us, "He that loves not knows not God; for God is love." By this scripture we know that our Father God is a God of love, that He is Love. This is the foundation of inner healing prayer. Knowing this, we can boldly ask our Lord to make Himself known to us or to our children in whatever moment of need. "God is our refuge and strength, a very present help in trouble" (Psalms 46:1). Because, He is Love, we can know something good is going to happen when we invite Him to be Lord of that moment.

Perhaps your children are already grown, but there were moments in their childhood when they needed to see or sense the Lord's Presence with them. It's not too late, you can still pray inner healing prayer for them. Remember God is outside of time, the past is still available to Him. Invite Him to come and take you back to those moments, give your children and that time to Him. Ask Him to be Lord over it. They do not need to know that you are praying inner healing for them in order for their hearts to be touched by God.

One woman with whom I prayed inner healing prayer was fearful about her son's conception for neither she nor her husband were with the Lord at that time. The conception happened out of lust, and she was afraid that the son's problems were stemming from this.

Because God is Love and He is outside of time, we could ask Him to go back to the time of conception and preside over the beautiful miracle of her child receiving his life. We asked the Lord to bless that moment for father, mother, and child and to make it holy. This He did, making known to the child that he was His child, that he was loved and wanted. Jesus brought peace not only for the moment, but His peace and healing to a mother's heart. Surprisingly enough, she began to hear from her son that his problems were being resolved. The mother never told her son about that prayer.

# My Journal

### DATE:

*Journal what you see the Lord doing or saying and how your child or children are responding.*

*For thou hast possessed my reins: thou hast covered me in my mother's womb. I will praise thee; for I am fearfully and wonderfully made: marvelous are thy works; and that my soul knoweth right well. My substance was not hid from thee, when I was made in secret, …Thine eyes did see my substance, yet being unperfect; and in thy book all my members were written, which in continuance were fashioned, when as yet there was none of them.*

—Psalms 139:13-16

You were written in God's book before you were in your mother's womb, and when you were there, He covered you with His love.

*Whither shall I go from thy spirit? Or whither shall I flee from thy presence? If I ascend into heaven, thou art there: if I make my bed in hell, behold, thou art there. If I take the wings of the morning, and dwell in the uttermost parts of the sea; Even there shall thy hand lead me, and thy right hand shall hold me. If I say, Surely the darkness shall cover me; even the night shall be light about me. Yea, the darkness hideth not from thee; but the night shineth as the day: the darkness and the light are both alike to thee.*

—Psalms 139:7-12

God is always with us, wherever we go, God is already there. Even in our darkest times, when our enemy and God's enemy, Satan was seeking to steal, kill, and destroy us; God was there. The enemy has a strategy of destruction for every human life, but Jesus came to destroy the works of the devil in our lives and give us life more abundantly. "For this purpose, the Son of God was manifested, that He might destroy the works of the devil" (1John 3:8, NKJV). "The thief comes not, but for to steal, and to kill, and to destroy: I am come that they might have life, and that they might have it more abundantly" (John 10:10).

When we pray inner healing prayer for ourselves or our children, we are inviting Jesus to enter that moment, and we are actually giving Him permission by our faith to be Lord of that time of our lives. He then allows us to live that moment again in our hearts, but this time the Holy Spirit is writing the script according to Father's will in Heaven. We then know and experience Father's will being enacted in whatever situation. The first time around the enemy wrote the script of destruction, the second time around Father's will is done on earth (in our hearts) as it is in Heaven.

Father's truth, the TRUTH, is eternal. Goodness and righteousness are forever, but all lies and evil will pass away and the Destroyer, Satan will himself be destroyed (Revelation 20:10). Jesus, who said, "I am the way, the truth, and the life…" John 14:6, sets us free from the effects of the lies, evil, or harm that Satan has caused us. We then do not have to fear evil, Psalms 23:4 says, "I will fear no evil, for thou art with me." Just as my son no longer had to fear; he saw Jesus with him, and Jesus was bigger than the man with the stick.

Luke 10:19 tells us, "Behold, I give you power…over all the power of the enemy: and nothing shall by any means hurt you.' This is Father's plan for us His children, that we are not hurt by the enemy nor anything else. Part of the fulfillment of this plan is the healing of our hearts through inner healing prayer.

*When you (God) said, "Seek my face," My heart said to You, "Your face, Lord, I will seek."*

—Psalms 27:8, NKJV

You are seeking His face in your inward being, in your heart when you pray inner healing prayer. It is His face, His countenance, His Presence that heals your broken heart.

**"Come Father, come Lord Jesus,
come Holy Spirit and
do that which you long to do,
heal our hearts."**

# ABOUT THE AUTHOR

Shade O'Driscoll, a graduate of Duke University, attended Union Theological Seminary, studying Old and New Testament, and Systematic Theology. She founded and taught a community Bible study in Northern Virginia.

Shade, as an Episcopal priest's wife, began inner healing prayer in their churches, and saw God heal hearts from sexual abuse, abortion, pornography, broken marriages, and more in His unrelenting love. She is the mother of six children.

*odriscollphoto.com*

# NOTES

## Chapter 4

1  Ruth Carter Stapleton, *The Gift of Inner Healing* (Waco, Texas: Word Incorporated, 1976).

## Chapter 7

2  Roxanne Brant, *Releasing God's Ideas by Praying in the Spirit* (Florida: Roxanne Brant Ministries Northern Florida Christian Center, Inc. O'Brian, 1985).

## Chapter 9

3  Rita Bennett, *You Can Be Emotionally Free.* (North Brunswick, New Jersey: Bridge-Logos Publishers, 1982).

CPSIA information can be obtained
at www.ICGtesting.com
Printed in the USA
JSHW051436170123
36214JS00002B/7